John Winston

A relic of the rebellion

What happened twenty-six years ago

John Winston

A relic of the rebellion
What happened twenty-six years ago

ISBN/EAN: 9783337243258

Printed in Europe, USA, Canada, Australia, Japan

Cover: Foto ©ninafisch / pixelio.de

More available books at **www.hansebooks.com**

A

Relic of the Rebellion

—OR,—

WHAT HAPPENED TWENTY-SIX YEARS AGO.

A true copy of THE NEW YORK HERALD, as published on the 15th of April, 1865, the morning after the Assassination of President Lincoln.

J. H. WINSTON,

215 E. 89TH ST., NEW YORK.

1891.

"A RELIC OF THE REBELLION" is the title of this little publication, it being, as stated hereinbefore, a reproduction of *The New York Herald*, relating the most important events of the Rebellion, which terminated twenty-six years ago.

To whatever extent this little volume may contribute to revive the interest in the past, I hope it will be a welcome guest to the American people, North and South, East and West.

The news of the Assassination of President Lincoln spread a mantle of grief over the entire nation and produced a general mourning as no similar event recorded in history has ever done before. Mr. Lincoln had during his administration achieved the respect and admiration of his country, besides gaining the universal, heartfelt sympathy of all. He was looked upon as the embodiment of all those features of our institutions which, theoretically, place all of our citizens on a political equality, and open the doors of the highest places of power and trust to the humblest amongst us.

This little work, though brief, will be found very instructive and interesting, as well to the aged as to the young; to the aged because it recalls facts they are acquainted with, instructive to the young because it relates facts they have heard of.

Feeling confident that all true Americans will accept this as a relic and a reminder of the direst event any nation ever bowed under, and hoping it may meet the approval of all, I cordially present it to the public.

J. H. WINSTON.

A Relic of the Rebellion.

IMPORTANT.

Assassination of President Lincoln:

The President Shot at the Theatre Last Evening.—Secretary Seward Daggered in His Bed, but Not Mortally Wounded.—Clarence and Frederick Seward Badly Hurt.—Escape of the Assassins.—Intense Excitement in Washington.—Scene at the Deathbed of Mr. Lincoln.—J. Wilkes Booth, the Actor, the Alleged Assassin of the President.—The Official Despatch.

WAR-DEPARTMENT,
WASHINGTON, April 15—1:30 A.M.

Major-General Dix, New York.—

This evening at about 9.30 P. M., at Ford's Theatre, the President, while sitting in his private box with Mrs. Lincoln, Mrs. Harris and Major Rathburn, was shot by an assassin, who suddenly entered the box and approached behind the president.

The assassin then leaped upon the stage, brandishing a large dagger or knife, and made his escape in the rear of the theatre.

The pistol ball entered the back of the President's head and penetrated nearly through the head. The wound is mortal.

The President has been insensible ever since it was inflicted, and is now dying.

About the same hour an assassin, whether the same or not, entered Mr. Seward's apartments, and under pretence of having a prescription was shown to the Secretary's sick chamber. The assassin immediately rushed to the bed and inflicted two or three stabs on the throat and two on the face.

It is hoped the wounds may not be mortal. My apprehension is that they will prove fatal.

The nurse alarmed Mr. Frederick Seward, who was in an adjoining room, and he hastened to the door of his father's room, when he met the assassin, who inflicted upon him one or more dangerous wounds. The recovery of Frederick Seward is doubtful.

It is not probable that the President will live through the night.

General Grant and wife were advertised to be at the theatre this evening, but he started to Burlington at six o'clock this evening.

At a Cabinet meeting, at which General Grant was present, the subject of the state of the country and the prospect of a speedy peace were discussed. The President was very cheerful and hopeful, and spoke very kindly of General Lee and others of the confederacy, and of the establishment of government in Virginia.

All the members of the Cabinet except Mr. Seward, are now in attendance upon the President.

I have seen Mr. Seward, but he and Frederick were both unconscious.

EDWIN M. STANTON,
Secretary of War.

THE HERALD DISPATCHES.

WASHINGTON, April 14, 1865.

Assassination has been inaugurated in Washington. The bowie knife and pistol have been applied to President Lincoln and Secretary Seward. The former was shot in the throat, while at Ford's theatre to-night. Mr. Seward was badly cut about the neck, while in his bed at his residence.

SECOND DISPATCH.

WASHINGTON, April 14, 1865.

An attempt was made about ten o'clock this evening to assassinate the President and Secretary Seward. The President was shot at Ford's Theatre. Result not yet known. Mr. Seward's throat was cut, and his son badly wounded.

There is intense excitement here.

Details of the Assassination.

WASHINGTON, April 14, 1865.

Washington was thrown into an intense excitement a few minutes before eleven o'clock this evening, by the announcement that the President and Secretary Seward had been assassinated and were dead.

The wildest excitement prevailed in all parts of the city. Men, women and children, old and young, rushed to and fro, and the rumors were magnified until we had nearly every member of the Cabinet killed. Some time elapsed before authentic data could be ascertained in regard to the affair.

The President and Mrs. Lincoln were at Ford's theatre, listening to the performance of the American cousin, occupying a box in the second tier. At the close of the third act a person entered the box occupied by the President, and shot Mr. Lincoln in the head. The shot entered the back of his head, came out above the temple.

The assassin then jumped from the box upon the stage and ran across to the other side, exhibiting a dagger in his hand, flourishing it in a tragical manner, shouting the same words repeated by the desperado at Mr. Seward's house, adding to it, "The South is avenged," and then escaped from the back entrance to the stage, but in his passage dropped his pistol and his hat.

Mr. Lincoln fell forward from his seat, and Mrs. Lincoln fainted.

The moment the astonished audience could realize what had happened, the President was taken and carried to Mr. Peterson's house, in Tenth street, opposite to the theatre. Medical aid was immediately sent for, and the wound was at first supposed to be fatal, and it was announced that he could not live, but at half-past twelve he is still alive, though in a precarious condition.

As the assassin ran across the stage, Colonel J. B. Steward, of this city, who was occupying one of the front seats in the orchestra, on the same side of the house as the box occupied by Mr. Lincoln, sprang to the stage and followed him; but he was obstructed in his passage across the stage by the fright of the actors, and reached the back-door about three seconds after the assassin had passed out. Colonel Steward got to the street just in time to see him mount his horse and ride away.

This operation shows that the

whole thing was a preconcerted plan. The person who fired the pistol was a man about thirty years of age, about five feet nine, spare built, fair skin, dark hair, apparently bushy, with a large mustache. Laura Keene and the leader of the orchestra declare that they recognized him as J. Wilkes, the actor, and a rabid secessionist. Whoever he was, it is plainly evident that he thoroughly understood the theatre and all its approaches and modes of escape to the stage. A person not familiar with the theatre could not have possibly made his escape so well and quickly.

The alarm was sounded in every quarter. Mr. Stanton was notified, and immediately left his house.

All the other members of the Cabinet escaped attack.

Cavalrymen were sent out in all directions, and dispatches sent to all the fortifications, and it is thought they will be captured.

About half past ten o'clock this evening a tall, well dressed man made his appearance at Secretary Seward's residence, and applied for admission. He was refused admission by the servant, when the desperado stated that he had a prescription from the Surgeon General, and that he was ordered to deliver it in person. He was still refused, except upon the written order of the physician. This he pretended to show, and pushed by the servant and rushed up stairs to Mr. Seward's room. He was met at the door by Mr. Fred. Seward, who notified him that he was master of the house, and would take charge

of the prescription. After a few words had passed between them, he dodged by Fred. Seward and rushed to the Secretary's bed, and struck him in the neck with a dagger, and also in the breast.

It was supposed at first that Mr. Seward was killed instantly, but it was found afterwards that the wound was not mortal.

Major Wm. H. Seward, Jr., paymaster, was in the room, and rushed to the defence of his father, and was badly cut in the *melee* with the assassin, but not fatally.

The desperado managed to escape from the house, and was prepared for escape by having a horse at the door. He immediately mounted his horse, and sung out the motto of the State of Virginia, "*Sic Semper Tyrannis!*" and rode off.

Surgeon General Barnes was immediately sent for, and he *examined Mr. Seward and pronounced him safe.* His wounds were not fatal. The jugular vein was not cut, nor the wound in the breast deep enough to be fatal.

WASHINGTON, April 15—1 A. M.

The streets in the vicinity of Ford's Theatre are densely crowded by an anxious and excited crowd. A guard has been placed across Tenth street and F and E streets, and only official persons and particular friends of the President are allowed to pass.

The popular heart is deeply stirred and the deepest indignation against leading rebels is freely expressed.

The scene at the house where the

President lies *in extremis* is very affecting. Even Secretary Stanton is affected to tears.

When the news spread through the city that the President had been shot, the people, with pale faces and compressed lips, crowded every place where there was the slightest chance of obtaining information in regard to the affair.

After the President was shot, Lieutenant Rathburn caught the assasin by the arm, who immediately struck him with a knife, and jumped from the box as before stated.

The popular affection for Mr. Lincoln has been shown by this diabolical assassination, which will bring eternal infamy, not only upon its authors, but upon the hellish cause which they desire to avenge.

Vice-President Johnson arrived at the White House, where the President lies, about one o'clock, and will remain with him to the last.

The President's family are in attendance upon him also.

As soon as intelligence could be got to the War Department, the electric Telegraph and Signal corps were put in requisition to endeavor to prevent the escape of the assassins, and all the troops around Washington are under arms.

Popular report points to a somewhat celebrated actor of known secession proclivities as the assassin; but it would be unjust to name him until further evidence of his guilt is obtained. It is rumored that the person alluded to is in custody.

The latest advices from Secretary Seward reveals more desperate work there than at first supposed. Seward's wounds are not in themselves fatal, but, in connection with his recent injuries, and the great loss of blood he has sustained, his recovery is questionable.

It was Clarence A. Seward, instead of Wm. H. Seward, Jr., who was wounded. Fred. Seward was also badly cut, as were also three nurses, who were in attendance upon the Secretary, showing that a desperate struggle took place there. The wounds of the whole party were dressed.

ONE O'CLOCK A. M.

The President is perfectly senseless, and there is not the slightest hope of his surviving. Physicians believe that he will die before morning. All of his Cabinet, except Secretary Seward, are with him. Speaker Colfax, Senator Farwell, of Maine, and many other gentlemen, are also at the house awaiting the termination.

The scene at the President's bedside is described by one who witnessed it as most affecting. It was surrounded by his Cabinet ministers, all of whom were bathed in tears, not even excepting Mr. Stanton, who, when informed by Surgeon General Barnes that the President could not live until morning, exclaimed, "Oh, no, General, no—no;" and with an impulse natural as it was unaffected, immediately set down on a chair near his bedside and wept like a child.

Senator Sumner was seated on the right of the President's couch, near the head, holding the right hand of the President in his own.

He was sobbing like a woman, with his head bowed down almost on the edge of the bed on which the President was lying.

TWO O'CLOCK A. M.

The President is still alive, but there is no improvement in his condition.

THE PRESS DESPATCHES.

WASHINGTON, April 15—1 A. M.

The President was shot in a theatre to-night, and is perhaps mortally wounded.

SECOND DESPATCH.

WASHINGTON, April 15—1 A. M.

The President is not expected to live through the night. He was shot at the theatre.

Secretary Seward was also assassinated. No arteries were cut.

Additional Details of the Assassination.

WASHINGTON, April 15—1.30 A. M.

President Lincoln and wife, with other friends this evening visited Ford's Theatre, for the purpose of witnessing the performance of the American cousin.

It was announced in the papers that General Grant would also be present; but that gentleman took the late train of cars for New Jersey.

The theatre was densely crowded, and all seemed delighted with the scene before them. During the third act, and while there was a temporary pause for one of the actors to enter, a sharp report of a pistol was heard, which merely attracted attention, but suggested nothing serious, until a man rushed to the front of the President's box, waving a long dagger in his right hand, and exclaiming, " *Sic semper tyrannis*," and immediately leaped from the box, which was on the second tier, to the stage beneath, and ran across to the opposite side, making his escape, amid the bewildered state of the audience, from the rear of the theatre, and mounting a horse, fled.

The screams of Mrs. Lincoln first disclosed the fact to the audience that the President had been shot, when all present rose to their feet, rushing towards the stage, many exclaiming "Hang him! Hang him!"

The excitement was of the wildest possible description, and, of course, there was an abrupt termination of the theatrical performance.

There was a rush toward the President's box, when cries were heard:—" Stand back and give him air." " Has any one stimulants?"

On a hasty examination it was found that the President had been shot through the head above and back of the temporal bone, and that some of the brain was oozing out.

He was removed to a private house opposite the theatre, and the Surgeon General of the army and other surgeons were sent for to attend to his condition.

On an examination of the private box blood was discovered on the back of the cushioned rocking chair on which the President had been sitting, also on the partition and on the floor. A common single-barrelled pocket pistol was found on the carpet.

A military guard was placed in front of the private residence to which the President had been conveyed. An immense crowd was in front of it, all deeply anxious to learn the condition of the President. It had been previously announced that the wound was mortal, but all hoped otherwise. The shock to the community was terrible.

At midnight the Cabinet, with Messrs. Sumner, Colfax and Farnsworth, Judge Curtis, Governor Oglesby, General Meigs, Colonel Hay, and a few personal friends, with Surgeon General and his immediate assistants, were around his bedside.

The President was in a state of syncope, totally insensible, and breathing slowly. The blood oozed from the wound at the back of his head.

The surgeons exhausted every possible effort of medicinal skill, but all hope was gone.

The parting of his family with the dying President is too sad for description.

The President and Mrs. Lincoln did not start for the theatre until fifteen minutes after eight o'clock. Speaker Colfax was at the White House at the time, and the President stated to him that he was going. Mrs. Lincoln had not been well, because the papers had announced that General Grant and they were to be present, and, as General Grant had gone North, he did not wish the audience to be disappointed.

He went with apparent reluctance, and urged Mr. Colfax to go with him, but that gentleman had made other engagements, and with Mr. Ashmun, of Massachusetts, bid him goodby.

When the excitement at the theatre was at its wildest height reports were circulated that Secretary Seward had also been assassinated.

On reaching this gentleman's residence a crowd and a military guard were found at the door, and on entering it was ascertained that the reports were based on truth.

Everybody there was so excited that scarcely an intelligible word could be gathered. But the facts are substantially as follows:—

About ten o'clock a man rang the bell, and the call having been answered by a colored servant, he said he had come from Dr. Verdi, Secretary Seward's family physician, with a prescription, at the same time holding in his hand a small piece of folded paper, and saying, in answer to a refusal, that he must see the Secretary, as he was entrusted with particular directions concerning the medicine.

He still insisted on going up, although repeatedly informed that no one could enter the chamber. The man pushed the servant aside, and walked hastily towards the Secretary's room, and was then met by Mr. Frederick Seward, of whom he demanded to see the Secretary, making the same representation which he did to the servant.

What further passed in the way of colloquy is not known; but the man struck him on the head with a billy, severely injuring the skull and felling him almost senseless.

The assassin then rushed into the chamber and attacked Major Seward, Paymaster United States

Army, and Mr. Hansell, a messenger of the State Department, and two male nurses, disabling them all.

He then rushed upon the Secretary, who was lying in bed in the same room, and inflicted three stabs in the neck, but severing, it is thought and hoped, no arteries, though he bled profusely.

The assassin then rushed down stairs, mounted his horse at the door, and rode off before an alarm could be sounded and in the same manner as the assassin of the President.

It is believed that the injuries of the Secretary are not fatal, nor those of either of the others, although both the Secretary and the Assistant Secretary are very seriously injured.

Secretary Stanton and Wellee, and other prominent officers of the Government called at Secretary Seward's house to inquire into his condition and there heard of the assassination of the President.

They then proceeded to the house, where he was lying, exhibiting of course intense anxiety and solicitude. An immense crowd was gathered in front of the President's house, and a strong guard was also stationed there. Many persons evidently supposing he would be brought to his home.

The entire city to-night presents a scene of wild excitement, accompanied by violent expressions of indignation and the profoundest sorrow ; many shed tears.

The military authorities have despatched mounted patrols in every direction, in order, if possible, to arrest the assassins. The whole metropolitan police are likewise vigilant for the same purpose.

The attacks, both at the theatre and at Secretary Seward's house, took place at about the same hour— ten o'clock—thus showing a preconcerted plan to assassinate those gentlemen. Some evidences of the guilt of the party who attacked the President are in the possession of the police.

Vice-President Johnson is in the city and his headquarters are guarded by troops.

THE STATE CAPITAL

Rejection of the New York Fire Commissioners.—Passage of the Central Railroad Fair Bill.—Great Excitement Over the Health Bill, &c.

ALBANY, April 14—11.40 P. M.

Legislation each day is now so rapid here that a detail or analysis of its progress is out of the question. To-day the long pending Central Railroad bill passed the Senate, and is virtually a law if the Governor does not veto it. But the result may be forshadowed in the veto sent in to-day of the Dry Dock and Battery Railroad.

The Health bill, which two days since was bound by caucus rules to have a sure passage, was to-night defeated by Republican votes. The Collector of the port of New York, who has had an elaborate organization up for his retention in the office of Commissioner of Charities, was thrown overboard and the power of all his patronage disregarded in the strife to secure this position which has been his pet desire and special-

ty for many years. All these oc-
currences have a political signifi-
cancy which it would take too
much time and space to develop.
The excitement of the day has been
the Health bill, and that excitement has been so incoherent as to
be indescribable. The attempt made
last night to kill off the bill was renewed to-day at an early hour. It
has been lost for want of a sufficient
vote, and laid on the table for reconsideration. A motion was made
to call it up for a final vote a short
time after the reading of the
Journal, by its opponents. The
tactics against the measure were
led by Weed, of Clinton, in whose
fresh abilities the democrats have
gained their ablest accession in this
Legislature. He moved to take
from the table, and upon that the
previous question. The vote of
fifty-three to sixty-one disclosed the
fact that the friends of the bill were
in the minority, and a panic at once
was created among them. An
adroit suggestion was sent to the
Speaker—understood to be from
Henry J. Raymond who was on the
floor—to rule that his vote did not
carry the bill, and another must be
taken. Mr. Van Buren, of New
York, moved to adjourn, which the
Speaker overruled amidst the
greatest uproar, Weed and others
insisting that such an action was
out of order.

While the vote was being taken a
few more republicans were drum-
med up, and the motion carried by
one or two votes. Hereupon the
wildest scenes of confusion took
place, all the members gathered in
a crowd before the Speaker's desk
in the most excited condition, shouting, disputing and threatening
each other and the Speaker. One
member from New York got upon a
desk, and in the midst of a clamor
for bets, offered at a thousand dollars, shouted and taunted the republicans, daring any man to bet.
He shook his two fists with hands-
full of greenbacks. Others clamored
in like manner, and the scene re-
sembled the most exciting days at
the gold room in New York. In
the midst of all this were heard the
clapping of hands and the triumph-
ant imitations of the mock chanti-
cleer of the republicans, while the
democrats uttered the most violent
denunciations of the Speaker to
his face for his rulings.

This scene was disposed of only
to be reproduced for the evening
session. Mr. Weed renewed his
assaults upon the bill to bring it to
a final vote, while its diminished
friends sought to postpone this
action. Messrs. Van Buren, Stuart,
Reed, Brandreth, Wood and Parker
sought alternately to postpone or
to kill time by filibustering, after
prolonged, excited and most dis-
orderly proceedings.

A final vote was forced upon the
friends of the bill at a late hour.
Sixty-one voted for the bill and
fifty-one against it. Sixty-five
votes being necessary to its passage, it was lost. Mr. Salmon, of
New York, who had made himself
obnoxious by the vehemency of his
opposition to the bill, was sought
to be involved in proceedings
before the bar of the House; but
the Speaker was evidently discour-
aged from any such attempts. The

management for the bill on the floor of the House was understood to be in the hands of the radicals, under the lead of Fields. Boole was in the lobby in person. Mayor Gunther, Carr and others of his opponents were here yesterday to urge on the passage of the bill. It is alleged that the Republican interest was sold out by the Radicals.

The Fire Commissioners encountered a decided capsize in executive session. The defeat of the Health bill was pending on their consideration, and the Assembly had adjourned in the extraordinary manner of the morning. The names were at first confirmed, Senator Laimbier, who had made the chief opposition, moving the confirmation. This action was, however, reconsidered on motion of Senator Andrews, on the ground of the promises made in the Assembly to the democrats, who passed it, that the board would comprise two democrats. The names were accordingly sent back to the Governor.

The continuation of Boole in office by the defeat of the Health bill is accompanied by the passage of a resolution continuing the Senate investigating committee, to sit during the summer and examine the other departments. The feeling here is that Boole was treated as an invidious exception and the thing will be made even all round.

The action determined on in caucus yesterday in regard to Draper and the Board of Charities, was desked by resolution to-day, and is coupled with the defeat of

Rufus F. Andrews as candidate for United States District Attorney at New York, as a satisfactory manifestation of Thurlow Weed's power.

The passage of the Central Railroad Fare bill was conducted through the form of third reading with no excitement, and with the limit of seven per cent. dividends. The increase of half a cent per mile for three years is thought only reasonable.

IMPORTANT FROM SOUTH AMERICA.

Surrender of Montevideo to Gen. Flores.—Brazil in the Possession of the City, &c.

The Brazilian mail arrived at Lisbon April 2, bringing the following advices:—

Montevideo has surrendered to General Flores.

The Brazilians now (March 11) occupy the city.

RIO JANEIRO, March 11, 1865.
Exchange 25⅜ a 26¼.

Coffee — Sales of good firsts at 65.66. Shipments, 100,000 bags. Stock, 100,000 bags. Freights, 50.62½.

BAHIA, March 11, 1865.
Exchange 26¼. Cotton nominal.

PERNAMBUCO, March 11, 1865.
Exchange 26½ a 27.

News from San Francisco.

SAN FRANCISCO, April 12, 1865.
The exports of treasure for the quarter just ended show a falling off of about six and a half millions as compared with the same period last year.

SAN FRANCISCO, April 14, 1865.
The Pacific Mail Steamship Sacramento sailed to-day, with a

large number of passengers for New York, and $1,153,000 in treasure, of which nearly $700,000 go to New York.

The steamship Moses Taylor sailed for San Juan del Sur with numerous passengers.

The market continues variable and unsettled, and traders pursue a continuous policy. Prices of Eastern goods are slowly falling.

Sailed, ship Flying Eagle, for Boston.

New Orleans Markets.

NEW ORLEANS, April 8,
Via CAIRO, April 14, 1865.

The New Orleans markets are at a stand still. Low middling cotton is quoted at 42c. per pound, and good superfine flour at $9 per barrel.

THE REBELS.

Jeff. Davis at Danville:—His Latest Appeal to His Deluded Followers.— He Thinks the Fall| of Richmond a Blessing in Disguise, as It Leaves the Rebel Armies Free to Move from Point to Point.—He Vainly Promises to Hold Virginia at all Hazards.—Lee and His Army Supposed to Be Safe.—Breckinridge and the Rest of Davis's Cabinet Reach Danville Safely.—The Organ of Governor Vance, of North Carolina, Advises the Submission of the Rebels to President Lincoln's Terms, &c., &c.

Jeff. Davis' Last Proclamation.

VIRGINIA TO BE HELD BY THE REBELS AT ALL HAZARDS.

DANVILLE, Va., April 5, 1865.

The General-in-Chief found it necessary to make such movements of his troops as to uncover the capital. It would be unwise to conceal the *moral and material injury to our cause* *resulting from the occupation of our capital* by the enemy. It is equally unwise and unworthy of us to allow our own energies to falter and our efforts to become relaxed under adverses, however calamitous they may be. For many months *the largest and finest army* of the Confederacy, under command of a leader whose presence inspires equal confidence in the troops and the people, has been greatly trammelled by the necessity of keeping constant watch over the approaches to the capital, and has thus been forced to forego more than one opportunity for promising enterprise. It is for us, my countrymen, to show by our bearing under reverses how wretched has been the self-deception of those who have believed us less able to endure misfortune with fortitude than to encounter dangers with courage.

We have now entered upon a new phase of the struggle. Relieved from the necessity of guarding particular points, *our army will be free to move from point to point* to strike the enemy in detail far from his base. *Let us but will it and we are free.*

Animated by that spirit and fortitude, which never yet failed me, I announce to you, fellow-countrymen, that it is my purpose to maintain your cause with my whole heart and soul, that I will never consent to the enemy one foot, the spoil of any one of the States of the confederacy, inflate at Virginia— noble State—whose ancient renown has been eclipsed by her still more glorious recent history; whose bosom has been bared to receive the main shock of this war; whose sons and daughters have exhibited heroism so sublime as to render her illustrious in all time to come—that Virginia, with the help of the people and by the blessing of Providence, *shall be held and defended*, and no peace ever be made with the infamous invaders of her territory.

If by the stress of numbers we should ever be compelled to a temporary withdrawal from her limits, or those of any other border State, again and again will we return, until the baffled and exhausted enemy shall abandon in despair his endless and impossible task of making slaves of a people resolved to be free.

Let us, then, not despond my countrymen; but, relying on God, meet the foe with fresh defiance and with unconquered and unconquerable hearts.

JEFFERSON DAVIS.

The Evacution of the Rebel Capital.

THE FIRST REBEL ACCOUNT OF HOW THE CITY WAS ABANDONED.

[From the Danville (Va.) Register, April 5.]

Persons who left the capital Sunday night and Monday morning represent that the scene which followed the evacuation of the city by our troops beggars description. To preserve order and protect the property of the citizens who unavoidedly remained there, as far as could be done, the Nineteenth Virginia militia, under Colonel Evans, was placed on police duty in the city, to await the coming of the enemy; but accounts state that they failed to render any aid or protection to the people whatever. On Sunday night a mob of the lower classes of the city, composed, it is said, mostly of the foreign element, visited a number of the largest store-houses of the city and robbed them of their contents. It is affirmed that Main street was pillaged, and then burned, and that some of the milling establishments were also committed to the flames. We have no doubt that a considerable portion of that brave city has been laid in ashes, and a number of its people insulted, outraged, robbed and massacred. How painful the thought that the place should be given over to rapine and plunder, even before the public enemy entèred its limits. But the fact only proves that the people of Richmond have had secret enemies in their own midst scarcely less savage and even more treacherous and vindictive than the open foe.

We are told that the people banded together during the violent proceedings of the mob and resisted them with force, a street fighting ensuing, in which several persons were killed.

No intelligence has reached us of the enemy's troops occupying the city. The last trains of the Danville railroad, which came out of the place, left Monday morning, and passengers upon them had heard nothing from the enemy. The greater portion of Grant's army was transferred to the south side of James river some days ago, only the command of General Ord, which is composed mostly, if not entirely, of negro troops, being left on the north side. This command will enter and occupy the city. Some of our people who are acquainted with the character of General Ord think they have reason to hope that his treatment of the unfortunate people of Richmond will not be so hard, and cruel and inhuman as that which has fallen upon the heads of our fellow citizens in some other captured cities.

The newspapers of Richmond, we suppose, all fell into the hands of the enemy. The evacuation of the city was so sudden and unexpected —scarcely any one being prepared for it—that no time was left for the removal of so cumbrous an establishment as a city newspaper office. In a few days we may expect to hear that the *Enquirer*, or the *Whig*, or the *Examiner* is issued as a Yankee paper.

All the rolling stocks of the Richmond and Danville Railroad in running order was saved on the retreat from Richmond. A few old cars, not in a movable condition, were left at Manchester. No train was captured by the enemy near the junction, as was at one time reported; and, indeed, we do not believe that any body of Yankees had struck the road at any point up to yesterday evening.

The Secretary of War, the Quartermaster General, Commissary General and a number of other officers of the government, left Richmond on horseback, and will probably arrive at this place tomorrow.

Should General Lee establish his lines east of the junction, we suppose the State Legislature will be convened at Lynchburg.

All the specie and other valuables belonging to the banks in Richmond were removed from the city on Sunday, and have been carried to places of safety.

A considerable amount of goods purchased by the State for distribution to the people, we regret to learn, had to be left behind. Also the State archives remained in the city; but we perceive no motive the enemy can have in destroying them, as they will, no doubt, endeavor to occupy the city permanently, and establish a State government at Richmond under the federal Union.

Lee's Army Supposed to Be in a Safe Position.

[From the Raleigh Confederate, April 7.]

This is the time for rumor manufacturers who are engaged in a wholesale business. Sometimes they have it that whole brigades deserted in the last great battle; among others, Cook's brigade is selected as the bearer of the stigma. We are assured that such a statement has no foundation whatever; that no treachery induced the disaster at Petersburg, that our forces fought splendidly, and the enemy only succeeded by overwhelming numbers. We are convinced, too, from facts which we cannot mention, that *Lee's army is in a safe position* and that *his future movements will be directed with the skill and energy which distinguish this great captain.*

Having anticipated the probable loss of Richmond, and fully recognizing the importance of the disaster, we are, nevertheless, not of the number of those who give up the cause. In the Southern confederacy this day there is military strength of men, material and supplies to make independence certain. It is with the *people themselves* whether they secure or lose their liberties.

Rebel Particulars of the Battle at Petersburgh.

[From the Raleigh Confederate, April 7.]

An officer who left Richmond at nine o'clock on Monday morning last, informs us that at the time he left the city was in flames from Cary to Canal streets. The Shokoe warehouse and other entreports of supplies were burning. The bridges also had been fired.

No mob or violence of any kind had occurred up to the period when he left, so that the reports of a destructive mob on Sunday night are untrue. The enemy's cavalry entered the city as the train moved off that he came out in. The story of the mob, therefore, we hope, is entirely erroneous.

This officer describes the fighting on Saturday as terrific beyond description. The enemy forced column after column on our works, lapping our lines on the extreme right. They came nine columns deep. Eight lines faltered and were broken by the obstinacy of our defences; but the ninth broke over our forces like a whirlwind. He says the destruction of the enemy was immense. Our loss, we think, consisted mainly in the prisoners taken by the enemy. All the prisoners whom we captured were drunk, having been prepared according to Yankee tactics for this dreadful ordeal. Lieutenant Gen-

eral A. P. Hill was certainly killed. General Fitz Lee was not killed as reported, nor General W. H. F. Lee. No general officer from North Carolina was killed, as far as is heard. On Monday Sheridan attacked Fitz Lee and was handsomely repulsed.

The Organ of Governor Vance, of North Carolina, Advising General Lee to Submit to Mr. Lincoln's Terms.

[From the Raleigh Confederate, April 7.]

The *Conservative* occasionally seems to fall into very mysterious hands, and to come under the control of an incomprehensible influence. On the day before yesterday that paper availed itself of a period of extreme reverse and disaster to renew the attempt to cast odium on a portion of our own citizens, which has been a favorite policy with its political leaders ever since the reverses began, and after it was no longer politic to claim that they "made the revolution." Yesterday it sends to the public a leader of still more extraordinary import. From what we comprehend of it, it seems to be *a distinct proposition to submit and surrender upon the terms proposed by Lincoln.* This has never yet, that we recollect of, been more distinctively proposed, even by journals whose loyalty has been called in question. The *Conservative* says:—"It is nonsense to propose to treat with the North with any expectation of the concession that the confederacy is a government," and hence, says the *Conservative,* "if our authorities are determined to force this condition upon the North as a basis of negotiation, then the North will never negotiate." What is this but sur-render? Not only surrender, but an assertion to the world that the defence of the last four years has been of a position which is one of sheer nonsense—one which the North "never could admit." We have not seen in this controversy so bold and unconditional a justification of the Northern invasion; for, if we sought to force a claim inconsistent with reason, and to demand an " ad-mission " which " is an absurdity in anything like government," and the North only resisted such claim and refused such admission, then we are in the wrong and the Yankee government is right, and the writer of the article to which we are reply-ing does well when he *advices Gen-eral Lee not to* " *block up his way, at the threshold, by presenting a basis to which he knows the enemy will not yield,*" but " to meet him on his own ground " as " the only way to open the nego-tiation." When we remember what " his own ground " is, upon which the *Conservative* proposes to meet the enemy, we may readily understand how much it is prepared to con-cede. " His own ground " measured the length of three propositions : submission to the laws and consti-tution of the United States, the laying down of our arms, and ac-quiescence in Lincoln's proclama-tions. This is the ground on which the author of the editorial desires General Lee to meet Lincoln and " secure a talk about peace." We have no idea that Governor Vance will support this idea; but it is very unfortunate that now, in the very moment when everything should be said to uphold the hopes and confi-dence of the army and people, such sentiments should obtain publica-tion in the organ of the Governor.

High Prices in an Overstocked Market.

[From the Raleigh Confederate, April 7.]

Our market, on the arrival of the Weldon train, on yesterday, *became overstocked* with shad ; *they went off slowly at $50 per pair.*

Exchange of the Rebel General Vance.

[From the Ashville (N. C.) News.]

The exchange of prisoners seems to go steadily on. We have seen a large number of our mountain boys, who have reached home after a protracted imprisonment. Among others we were gratified to meet Brigadier General R. B. Vance, who reached home some days since. He looks rather worsted by his long confinement, but, as usual with him, is full of life, cheerful and buoyant. The general is a great favorite of the people of this section, and everybody was glad to see him.

City Intelligence.

EASTER SUNDAY AT ST. ANN'S CHURCH. - The admirers of sacred music, made truly effective by a well trained choir, have an oppor-tunity of indulging their taste by repairing to St. Ann's church on Easter Sunday evening, the doors opening at seven, the concert begin-ning at eight. Three of the pieces are from Gordigiani, three from Rossini and one from each of the composers Verdi, Donizetti, Ver-rimst, Dachauer and Gounod. We need only mention the names of Signor Remi and Messrs. Schmitz,

Schubert and Dachauer to insure confidence in the vocal results. The ladies are quite distinguished for contralto and soprano execution, and no exertion will be spared to make the musical feast worthy of the day.

A NEW CHURCH.—An advertisement among our religious notices announces the opening of the new Church of the Holy Trinity, Madison avenue, corner of Forty-second street, on Sunday. Sermons will be preached at the three sessions by Rev. Dr. Tyng, of St. George's; Rev. Dr. Dyer, and the Rev. Stephen H. Tyng, Jr., the pastor of the church. It promises to be an occasion of great interest to residents on Murray Hill.

CROTON ACQUEDUCT CONTRACTS.—The following contracts have been issued by this department:—Laying crosswalks from southeast corner of Fifty-ninth street and Broadway to the junction of Broadway and Eighth avenue, Matthew Murray, $625. Cobble stone pavement in Hammond street, west of Thirteenth avenue, Christy Dowd, $1,896.80. Sewer in Forty-third street, from Lexington avenue to Fourth avenue, John Duffy, Jr. $1,913.50. Sewer in Forty-sixth street, from Eleventh avenue to seventy-five feet west of Tenth avenue, John Rourke, $5,223.50. Fifty-second street, sewer from Sixth to Seventh avenues, Joseph Moore, $4,880. Sewer to 125th street, from Fifth avenue through Manhattan street to Tenth avenue, James Cunningham, $22,941.35.

MISS EMMA HARDINGE delivers her able lecture on " Politics in the Pulpit " this evening, at Dodworth Hall. To test the lady's ability, any questions the audience desire to ask will be answered.

MAN DROWNED.—On the morning of the 13th instant a journeyman housepainter, whose name is believed to be Barnard Burns, was accidently drowned at Guntherville, Long Island. His body has not yet been claimed by his friends. Mr. J. B. Acker, of No. 9 Macdougal street, will give facilities to any one who can identify the corpse.

Assassination of President Lincoln and Attempt to Assassinate Secretary Seward.

An unlooked for and terrible calamity has befallen the nation. President Lincoln last night received a wound at the hands of an assassin, the effects of which there are no hopes of his surviving, having been shot while sitting in a theatre witnessing the performance of a play. An attempt was also made, apparently by the same person who shot the President, to take the life of Secretary Seward. The assassin, after firing on the President, rushed in front of the box occupied by the latter, and waving a long dagger which he held in his right hand, exclaimed, using the motto of the State of Virginia, " Sic Semper Tyrannis ! " He then jumped on the stage, and, amidst the intense excitement which ensued, escaped through the rear of the building. The President was shot through the head. He was immediately removed, and on examining the wound the brain was found to be oozing therefrom. The best surgical skill was instantly summoned; but it was not thought it could be of any avail towards saving Mr. Lincoln's life. He was still living at an early hour this morning; but the last melancholy parting scene between himself and his family had taken place, and his death was momentarily looked for.

The attempt to assassinate Secretary Seward was made at an earlier hour in the evening than the attack on the President. The assailant forced his way into the sick chamber where Mr. Seward was confined to his bed, and, after dealing disabling blows on the attendants, rushed to the bedside and stabbed the Secretary in the neck and breast. He then fled from the house, mounted a horse and escaped, making use, as he did so, of the same exclamation used in the case of the President's assassination—"*Sic Semper Tyrannis!*" Though the wounds inflicted on Mr. Seward are not of a mortal character, it is feared that, owing to his previous debilitated condition, they may lead to fatal results.

The assassin had not been arrested up to the hour of our latest despatches. Who he is is not positively known, though suspicion points strongly to a certain individual.

THE SITUATION.

General Sherman's army commenced its advance from Goldsboro, N. C., on the 9th inst. It moves in three columns, commanded respectively by Generals Howard, Slocum and Schofield. General Schofield moved on the 9th, and the remainder on the following day. During the rejoicings over the capture of Richmond, previous to taking up the line of march, General Sherman was called out by his troops, and made a short speech, telling them to prepare to press forward, as no rest was to be given to Johnston. General Johnston's army had evacuated Raleigh, moving to the west of it, leaving the town in possession of four or five thousand of Hampton's cavalry. It was reported that Johnston had gone to Greensboro, at the junction of the Danville and Charlotte Railroads. On the evening of the 10th inst. a small force of General Howard's mounted infantry were attacked by some rebel cavalry, who, however, were soon dispersed, with a loss of one hundred men and two pieces of artillery.

It was reported in Goldsboro, N. C., on the 7th inst. that Governor Vance would soon call the North Carolina Legislature together to repeal the secession ordinance and restore the State to the Union.

Jeff. Davis, the errant President of the late rebel confederacy, has at last been decisively heard from. On the 5th inst., he issued from Danville, Va., a proclamation, which we publish this morning. He says that, General Lee, having "found it necessary to make such movements of his troops as to uncover" Richmond, "it would be unwise to conceal the moral and material injury" resulting to the rebel cause from its occupation by the national troops. Still he endeavors to convince his deluded followers that even this event is a "blessing in disguise," as it would liberate Lee's army for more important operations. He announces his purpose to still maintain his bad cause with his "whole heart and soul," and to "never submit to the abandonment of one State of the confederacy. "Virginia," he declares, "shall be held and defended, and no peace ever be made with the infamous invaders of her territory." Probably ere this, on learning of the surrender of General Lee, Jeff. has become willing to slightly modify this proclamation.

The capture of Selma, Alabama, by General Wilson's cavalry is confirmed from rebel sources. Mobile papers of the 4th inst. announced that it had been taken, with twenty-three pieces of artillery and a large amount of government property.

A New Orleans dispatch states that a furious fire was opened on the rebel works defending Mobile on the night of the 4th inst., and that during its continuance a magazine was exploded in Spanish Fort; but the amount of damage done had not been ascertained. Affairs were quiet in the vicinity of Mobile on the 5th inst. Spanish Fort was still besieged by the troops of the Thirteenth and Sixteenth corps, under Generals Gordon Granger and A. J. Smith, while Fort Blakeley, another strong rebel work, six miles nearer the city, was invested by the Seventh corps, General Steele commanding. Two more Union gunboats, the tin-clads No. 48 and Rodolph, had been sunk by rebel torpedoes. On the former one man was killed and on the latter four were killed and fifteen wounded. Rebel communication between Spanish Fort and Mobile, as stated in Thursday's HERALD, was entirely cut off by the national army. General Thomas, with the Fourth corps and thirty-five thousand cavalry, was expected soon to appear in front of Mobile on the north side.

A somewhat confused rebel despatch of the 5th inst. from Augusta, Georgia, indicates that Alabama is being completely overrun by the national cavalry under General Wilson and other commanders, all moving in the direction of Mobile. On the 1st inst. they were represented to be in force near Montevello and Tuscaloosa. General McCook's force is reported to have burned Red Mountain Iron Works and the village of Elyton, and to have tapped the telegraph in several places and sent despatches to rebel officers. Two columns of Yankees were also represented to be advancing on Columbus, Mississippi, in the latter part of last month, one from Memphis and the other from Huntsville, Alabama. From the same despatch we learn that the rebel steamer Gertrude, with a cargo valued at two million dollars, was sunk in Spanish river, near Mobile, on the 31st ult., by colliding with the steamer Natchez, and proved a total loss.

President Lincoln yesterday ordered the revocation of the passes for the rebels Governor Letcher and Senator Hunter, to visit Richmond to take part in the proceedings for restoring Virginia to its proper position in the Union. It is said that the military officers in

Richmond granted these passes on insufficient authority.

Nearly four hundred and fifty captured rebel officers, including several generals, arrived in Washington yesterday. Among them was General Ewell.

Additional details of the ceremonies attending the surrender of General Lee's army are contained in the despatches of our correspondents published this morning.

The Danville (Va.) *Register* of the 5th inst., says that General Breckinridge, rebel Secretary of War; the rebel Quartermaster and Commissary Generals and a number of other officers, left Richmond on horseback just previous to its occupation by the national troops, and were expected to arrive in Danville on the 6th inst.

Four Union gunboats recently went up the Chowan river, in North Carolina, for the purpose of co-operating with some cavalry. At Winston a force of rebels was found; but they were soon dispersed by the shells from the gunboats, which ferried the cavalry across the stream and then proceeded to Murfreesboro, on the Meherrin river, which was also captured.

The ram which the rebels had been building at Halifax, N. C., and with which they expected to inflict great damage on the national vessels, was discovered in the river, above Plymouth, N. C., on the 8th inst., moving down; but she proved to be a mere shell, having been burned to the water's edge. The rebel ram Albemarle, sunk at Plymouth by Lieutenant Cushing and

his party, has been raised, and is found to be not seriously injured.

Orders to discontinue drafting and recruiting in the Southern division of this State, comprising the first ten Congressional districts, were yesterday received from Washington and transmitted to each of the district provost marshals. Business therefore came to a sudden termination at the Supervisors' rooms in the City Hall Park and at the several provost marshals' offices. Chairman Blunt, of the Volunteering Committee, had two hundred guns fired in honor of the event.

A Cairo despatch says that the rebel Colonel Forrest has arrived at Memphis under a flag of truce for the purpose of conferring with General Washburne on the subject of a proposed extermination of the guerillas.

EUROPEAN NEWS.

The steamship Europa, from Queenstown, April 2, arrived at Halifax yesterday morning, on her voyage to Boston. Her news is two days later.

The United States Minister at Lisbon had demanded satisfaction from the Portuguese government for the insult and injury done to our flag by firing on the Niagara and Sacramento. He requested that the commander of Fort Belem be dismissed and the Union flag saluted with twenty-one guns. No decision had been come to. The American commanders deny that they were about to sail before the appointed time, and say they were merely shifting their anchorage when fired on. Our special correspondence from Corunna gives an interesting narrative of the events which occurred to the date of the sailing of the Niagara and Sacramento from their anchorage off that place. The fact of eight guns having just been shipped from England to the Spanish coast increased the belief that there was another rebel privateer operating in the neighborhood. The remains of an American ship, burned to the water's edge, came ashore at Malpica, near Corunna.

The London *Times* correspondent in Richmond attempts to comfort the anglo-rebel sympathizers with the assurance that even if Lee and Johnston were defeated the " closing scene " of the war will trouble the United States during two or three generations.

The London *Times* condemns and ridicules the amended Tariff law of the United States.

A London journal pays a just tribute to the action of the United States Navy, under Farragut and Porter, during the war.

Consols closed in London, April 1, at 89⅞ a 90 for money. United States five-twenties were in brisk demand for the Continent. The value of the bonds experienced a slight relapse from the advance at the end of the week; but they again advanced to 57¾ to 58¼. The Bank of England reduced its rate of discount to four per cent.

Two failures in England—a commercial house and a bank—foot up liabilities of over one million sterling.

The Liverpool cotton market was weaker, but quiet, with prices unchanged, on April 1. Breadstuffs were quiet and steady. Provisions were quiet and steady.

THE LEGISLATURE.

In the Senate yesterday Mr. Munger, of the select committee appointed to investigate charges made against certain departments of our city government, reported that the committee was not yet able to make a written report, and asked that they be allowed to continue the investigation during the recess, and that their powers be extended so as to include all the departments in the city. This report was laid on the table. A message was received from the Governor vetoing the Dry Dock, East Broadway and North River Railroad bill, which was ordered to be printed. The Annual Supply bill was reported and made the special order for the evening session. The bill to increase the fare on the New York Central Railroad was then taken up and amended so as to prevent discrimination in favor of through freight and against way freight. It was then read and passed by a vote of yeas 18, nays 14. Bills were also adopted relative to the Croton Acqueduct in New York, and to incorporate the Harry Howard Association of Exempt Firemen. The Governor's nominees for Metropolitan Fire Commissioners were rejected in executive session by a vote of yeas 15, nays 17.

In the Assembly bills were reported for the erection of a new Capitol; to provide grounds for a final resting place of the remains of

New York Volunteeers who fell at Gettysburg and Antietam, and to change the name of the Mariners' Saving Institute. Mr. Weed moved to take from the table the Metropolitan Health bill, which was carried by a vote of yeas 53, nays 51. The question of the reconsideration of the vote by which the bill was lost was reached in evening session. When the result was announced, the bill was declared lost by a vote of ayes 52, nays 59.

MISCELLANEOUS NEWS.

South American advices, dated to the 11th of March, received, via England, by the steamship Europa, report the surrender of the city of Montevideo to General Flores. The Brazilians were in possession of the place. This confirms the statements given in the HERALD of the 8th and 12th inst.

The Cunard steamship Asia reached Halifax from Boston at half past eleven P. M. on Thursday, and sailed for Liverpool at three o'clock A. M. yesterday.

The steamship Corsica from Havana on the 8th, and Nassau on the 10th inst., arrived here yesterday. Her Havana advices are no later than those noticed in yesterday's HERALD. The Anglo-rebel blockade running steamship Banshee arrived at Nassau on the 30th ult., from Galveston, with one thousand bales of cotton. She reports twelve Union vessels off Galveston bar, and that the town is garrisoned by twelve hundred rebels. The French bark Eugene was wrecked on Great Inagua on the 25th of February, and three of her crew were drowned. When the Corsica was about four hours from this port some alcohol was exploded in the hold of the ship from the blaze of a candle, by which two persons were killed and three others seriously injured.

A New Orleans journal of the 8th inst. claimed to have intelligence that the commander of the principal army of Juarez in Central Mexico had abandoned the contest, and that his troops had returned to their homes.

President Lincoln has recently recognized Jose A. Codoy as consul of the Mexican republic at San Francisco, which fact would seem to be a contradiction of all the reports that our government designed acknowledging Maximilian's empire.

Yesterday, being Good Friday, the anniversary of the crucifixion of the Saviour, there were appropriate religious services in a large number of our city churches and a considerable suspension of business.

The law courts adjourned yesterday in honor of Good Friday. Orders returnable yesterday will be attended to to-day in chambers.

Yesterday Colonel Baker's detectives arrested J. W. Smalley, who had just returned from Charleston. He was the agent of Walden & Willard, recently arrested and sent to Washington on charge of defrauding sailors out of their prize money. Among the bounty brokers now in Fort Lafayette are William McAnauly, Michael Dillon, P. Goodman, D. P. Sullivan and J. F. Pike. Among those released are P. J. Kiernan, Jas. Thomson, Michael McNamara, Michael Fay,

A. Hiller, John Kelly, A. Higgins, S. J. Boyle, John Nugent and John Callan.

There were fourteen wills admitted to probate last week by Surrogate Tucker. Among them was that of William B. Crosty, in which five hundred dollars are given to the Sunday School of the Dutch Reformed Church in Market street.

The steamship Etna, Captain McGuigan, of the Inman line, will sail at noon to-day for Queenstown and Liverpool. The Teutonia, for Southampton and Hamburg, also sails to-day. The mails will close at half past ten A. M. at the post office.

Captain Powell, of the steamer Commander, arrived at this port yesterday from Morehead City, states that when off Cape Hatteras, on the 11th inst., he passed ten or twelve dead bodies floating on the water, which were supposed to be some of those lost when the steamer General Lyon was destroyed by fire. In yesterday's HERALD was noticed the fact of floating bodies having been seen in the same vicinity, on the same day, by the captain of the steamship Suwanee.

John Lehon, a wine merchant, and Christian Schutz, a jeweler, were yesterday committed to the Tombs for trial, on the charge of having attempted to burn the premises, No. 117 William street, on the night of the 9th inst. Schutz, after his arrest, made a confession, acknowledging his complicity in the affair.

There was no session of either of the stock boards or the Gold Exchange yesterday. Stocks were, however, firm on the street, and gold closed steady at 146.

Commercial matters were unusually quiet yesterday, and the day was more generally observed as a religious holiday than we ever knew Good Friday to be before. Business was very quiet, and there was a general disinclination to do anything until the country shall have been restored to something like order. On 'Change flour was dull, but prices were without material change. Wheat was firmer for spring, but dull and heavy for winter. Corn was firm and in limited supply. Oats were also scarce, and 1c. higher. Pork was in improved demand and firmer. Beef ruled steady. Lard was quiet but firm, while whiskey was decidedly lower and less active. Freights were dull and sales were nominal.

A Proclamation from Jeff. Davis.— His "Voice Is Still for War."

Jeff. Davis has turned up again. He has issued a proclamation from Danville, and his "voice is still for war." The reader will find that proclamation in another part of this paper. It is savage, sanguinary and defiant, from the first to the last; but it was issued upon the false presumption that, though he had lost Richmond, General Lee had escaped with his army. This absurdly belligerent edict is dated Danville, April 5, several days before the surrender of Lee, and doubtless before any information had reached Danville of the accumulating and fatal disasters of his awful retreat.

Under this delusive idea, however, that he still had Lee's army to support him, Davis defiantly falls back upon the strategy of Ben Wood. "The finest army of the confederacy, under its ablest military leader, had been greatly trammelled," he says, "by the necessity of keeping constant watch over the approaches to the capital," and thus it had been "forced to forego more than one opportunity for promising enterprises." In other words General Grant had driven this "finest army of the confederacy" into Richmond and then turned the key on it till ready to draw General Lee out, and then run him down. But, although Davis "can not conceal the moral and material injury" to his cause from the loss of his capital, he agrees with Ben Wood that his armies, "now relieved of the duty of guarding particular points, are free to move from point to point, and to strike the enemy in detail, far from his base," just as they struck Sherman, for instance, in his marches through Georgia, South and North Carolina.

Davis, at all events, declared that "Virginia shall be held and defended;" that he will "never abandon to the enemy one foot of the soil of any State of the confederacy;" but that if compelled to withdraw temporarily, he "will return, again and again, till the baffled and exhausted enemy shall abandon in despair his endless and impossible task of making slaves of a people resolved to be free." This was on the 5th of April, at Danville, and we dare say that by this time Davis, a little more enlightened, has abandoned

Virginia and North and South Carolina, and is perhaps meditating at Augusta, Ga., upon the safest route, via Texas, to Mexico.

It is possible, however, that the mad ambition and the terrible disappointments and misfortunes that have fallen upon this unhappy man have rendered him utterly reckless in his despair. If so, he will probably persist in his madness till stopped in a violent and ignominious death. But we cannot imagine that he has become so completely deranged. We rather incline to think that there is "a method in his madness"—something of strategy, to cover up his real designs, and to get safely off without exciting dangerous suspicions among his followers till well out of the way of danger.

In this view of his declared purposes of war to the death, we shall not be surprised if we do not hear directly from him again this side of the Mississippi river or the island of Cuba. Clearly he is not in the mood to accept a pardon; nor do we think that he seeks the unpleasant alternative threatened him of that "sour apple tree"—

As we go marching on.

Davis, in short, must have had some misgivings of Sheridan's cavalry, and, as we conjecture, he only stopped at Danville to hurl back upon "the Yankees" his last shout of wrath and defiance, and is off "for Cowes and a market."

SPAIN AND PORTUGAL AS NEUTRALS.—The attitude of Spain and Portugal in regard to this country, as evinced in their recent action towards the United States war vessels Niagara and Sacramento is decidedly hostile, and demands the immediate notice of our government. It has come to a pretty pass when such petty Powers can insult us with impunity. As for Portugal she has nothing to lose. Like a poor yelping dog, she scarcely merits a good kicking. But the case of Spain is quite different. She ought to remember that she has valuable possessions within easy reach of us. If we had sufficient cause to-morrow it would not require much more than a month to take Cuba and Porto Rico, and then Spanish pride and bombast would be brought rather low. Our government must look to this matter at once, and we trust that our representatives at Madrid and Lisbon will demand full and ample satisfaction. It is no excuse to say that these are weak Powers and of little importance. They must not be allowed to escape on any such pretence. Let them apologize at once, and promise better behavior in future, or be brought to an account.

The Revolutionary Effects of the War upon the Country.

No one can question that a grander development of this nation is to flow as a direct result from the war we have just passed through. Wars for national life and a great cause always develop, invigorate and inspirit a people, however small their power may be; and if they are finally crushed by such wars they go down a better and greater people than they were when the war began—a people higher in the social scale. But when such a war is waged on so stupendous a scale as our war has been, and by a people with so much intellectual and moral force, so much capability of growth, it cannot be but that the changes and progress that it must induce will be such as to belittle all the examples of the past and to revolutionize completely the present.

We believe that the influence in that way that the war is to have upon the country will amount to scarcely less than a new organization of our national life. Through all the future we will be a different people from that we have been. We have sloughed away in these few terrible years the forms of the older life, and already we are taking new ones with an imperative sense of what we are to be. Our national character grows larger in the contemplation of what we have done and by contact with great events. In the several years past Americans showed that the rudimentary freemen of the Revolutionary days, developing all the arts of peace, could be greater mechanics, inventors, traders and sailors than any other men; and now we have shown that Americans, taunted for their success in those arts and their love of the "almighty dollar" are possessed also of the grander manhood that succeeds in war; that they make also better soldiers than any other men, and that they can carry war to the same high pitch of development that they have carried so many other arts. The consciousness of this influence, the national mind and character, will stamp with a large and noble spirit the literature, history and philosophy that will grow out of it.

Our national industry and commerce will also feel this revolutionary effect, and vastly improved and enlarged commercial and better financial systems will be the result. The undaunted spirit of the navy will communicate itself to a mercantile marine that will make our flag familiar on every sea, and the world will derive new wealth from the fact that the attention of the people has for the first time fixed upon the great questions incident to the national finances. Industry, assuming a thousand new forms, will give us the full benefit of the untold resources of this great continent, and we shall be richer, more prosperous in all ways, more happy and more free than we ever were, or than any other people ever were. From the memorable epoch of the closing of this war the great revolution in our national life begins, and we take a fresh and glorious start.

THE ICE MONOPOLY.—We publish in another column a communication from the icedealers in reply to the notice we gave a few days since, informing the public that they had entered into a combination and decided to double their charges. We willingly give the answer in order that the public may see the weakness of their case. While almost everything of necessary consumption—such as flour, butter and provisions of all kinds, coal and wood, and cotton and woolen fabrics—is following, slowly we ad-mit, but surely and permanently, the decline of gold, it seems preposterous—and so the public will view it—that the ice dealers, in the face of such evidence, should now assume to double their last year's charges and quadruple the prices of four years ago. There are two facts in relation to the ice business which should not be lost sight of. One is that nature furnishes the dealers their stock in trade gratis, and the bountiful crop vouchsafed to them last winter leaves them no cause of complaint in that respect. And the other may be referred to as equally worthy of consideration. Congress, viewing ice as an article of necessity rather than luxury, relieved it from the burdens of the internal revenue law, and permitted the dealers to escape the direct tax, which has been placed upon almost every other commodity. But it is useless to present argument which is likely to stand in the way of combinations like that of the ice dealers. There can, therefore, be no harm in competition from Maine and Massachussets.

THE CRY FOR PROSCRIPTION.— Ben Butler and the radicals are calling out loudly for proscription, now that the war is over and the people generally, as well as the administration, are disposed to deal humanly with those who have erred and have been subdued. Mercy to a fallen foe is one of the highest characteristics of manhood; but it is one which Ben Butler and the radicals do not seem to regard. Their howling for proscription against the Southern people brings to our mind a few events of history—that excellent philosophy which teaches by example. It reminds us of Robespierre, who was the first to call for the guillotine in France, and who afterwards gave up his miserable life under it. It recalls, too, the story of Caius Marius, in the days of the Roman Republic, who demanded the proscription of the friends of Scylla, and subsequently perished in the marshes an outlaw and a fugitive. At that time the best men in Rome were proscribed, from which event dated the downfall of the republic. No good ever yet came from proscription. The spirit is wicked and unnatural. History is replete with instances to prove that the men who erect the guillotine are the first to suffer by it.

QUITE ANOTHER DODGE.—It was a singular instance of poetical justice that the same Dodge who wrote an insolent letter threatening to exact the last man from New York should be the very Dodge who telegraphed from Washington to stop the draft entirely. To us, however, this is quite another Dodge. The Major Dodge of the other day bullied us like a despot; the Major Dodge of this morning roars as gently as a sucking dove. It is astonishing what ups and downs there are in this great country, and how much more modest Lieutenant General Grant knows of the position of affairs than the thundering blundering Major Dodge.

ADVICE BY WAY OF POSTSCRIPT.—The other day we gave our last advice to Ben Wood; but as he still persists in writing himself down an ass, we add a postscript, and again say "don't." The Hon. Ben is foolish to pretend to get angry about the liberty of the press. His own existence and that of his paper are the best proofs that this liberty has not been invaded. We are very sorry that Ben feels so badly because peace has come; and we wonder at it, because he always professed to want peace. Perhaps he had better follow Jeff. Davis to Mexico, after all. Lotteries are fashionable there.

JOHN BROWN AND JEFF. DAVIS.—Some of the radical papers are crying for the blood of Jeff. Davis when he is caught. Remember Mrs. Glass's direction, "first catch your hare." Jeff. Davis is only a John Brown on a large scale; but to say that he deserves Brown's fate is not a strong argument in favor of hanging him. Brown went into Virginia, tried to raise a revolution, failed, and was hung; but his death did the country no good. Davis tried to raise a revolution, succeeded for a while, then failed; but if he be hung what good will it do the country? Let him die, like Benedict Arnold, in foreign lands, or go, like Judas, and hang himself.

MOBILE.

Fierce Bombardment of Spanish Fort.—Reported Loss of Two Tin-Clads.—Destruction of Rebel Transports.—The Continuance of the Siege, &c.. &c., &c.

New Orleans papers of the 6th inst. have been received. The

Times contains correspondence from our forces in front of Spanish Fort, Ala., to the 30th ult., and from Lakeport to the 4th inst. Siege guns and mortars are mounted by our forces near Spanish Fort, so as to almost, if not quite, cut off all rebel communication by land or water.

A rebel transport and hospital boat have been destroyed.

The Union tin-clad No. 48 was sunk by a torpedo and one man killed.

The *True Delta* has the report of the loss of the United States tin-clad Rodolph, by the explosion of a torpedo, while participating in the attack upon Spanish Fort. The correspondent states that two others (names not given) were blown up in a similar manner. Four persons were killed upon the Rodolph and fifteen wounded.

THE GRAND ATTACK

upon the rebel works was to have commenced on the 3d inst.

THE REBEL LOSS.

Another correspondent, from the same locality, under date of the 1st instant, writes:—

The military situation is very encouraging, although it has assumed the proportions of a regular siege.

By private advices, not yet confirmed, the rebel loss inside Spanish Fort is five hundred and fifty killed and wounded out of four thousand. Our total loss (an estimate of two corps) is probably the same. Proportion of killed small.

Brigadier General Mythe (a new man) is in command at the fort.

The rebel communication with Mobile is entirely suspended.

Steels (Seventh corps) is investing Fort Blakeley, six miles above Spanish Fort.

Thomas, with the Fourth corps and thirty-five thousand cavalry, is expected in the rear of Mobile. Nothing definite has been received from him for several days.

———

The Latest News.

NEW ORLEANS, April 8, }
    via CAIRO, April 14. }

A despatch in the New Orleans *Times* from Spanish Fort, dated April 5, says:—

A furious fire was opened on the rebel forts last night from our entire line. During the bombardment a small magazine in Spanish Fort exploded. The damage is unknown. Quiet prevailed on the 5th.

Deserters report from eighteen to twenty thousand troops in and about Mobile, including all the State reserves, and about two thousand in Spanish Fort.

The loss outside the Spanish Fort up to the 4th inst. amounted to about five hundred killed and wounded. The rebel loss exceeds ours.

Adjutant General Thomas arrived at New Orleans on the morning of the 7th.

Mobile papers of the 4th inst announced the capture of Selma, Alabama, with twenty-three pieces of artillery and a large amount of government property.

THE ALABAMA RAIDS.

Rebel Accounts of General Wilson's Movements on Selma and Montgomery.—Heavy Co-operating Column Moving Through Mississippi. —Affairs About Mobile. — The Wounding and Capture of General Clanton, &c.

AUGUSTA, April 5, 1865.

Western papers of late date represent the enemy as moving through the interior of Alabama in large force, from points on the Tennessee river. Two divisions are near Montevello, commanded by McCook.

The enemy are in force near Tuscaloosa.

Six thousand from Tuscumbia divided at Jasper—one column went to Tuscaloosa and the other towards Montevello. McCook's command was at Elyton on Tuesday, March 28. He had a large wagon train and artillery. He burned the village of Elyton and Red Mountain Iron Works. The enemy had tapped the telegraph wires at unknown points and despatched to Southern offices.

General Clanton despatched to his wife, March 28, that he was wounded seriously, and left by the enemy below Pollard, paroled by the Yankees. to report at Barancas on the 5th of April.

The *Clarion*, of the 27th, states that two columns of Yankees are advancing on Columbus, Mississippi. One from Huntsville had reached points thirty-five miles above Columbus. Another started from Memphis, four thousand strong, well provided with pack mules, and well mounted, and are in the vicinity of Pontotoc, Miss.

The steamers Gertrude and Natchez collided at the mouth of the Spanish river, near Mobile, at midnight, Friday, March 31. The Gertrude sunk in a few minutes. Cargo valued at two millions, and consisted of provisions, which belonged to citizens who had purchased to supply themselves for the siege of Mobile; total loss. The Natchez is uninjured.

Captain Vernon Lock, of the privateer Retribution, is in prison at Nassau.

BROADWAY THEATRE—LAST APPEARANCE OF MR. OWENS.—Mr. Owens will appear as Caleb Plummer, in the Cricket on the Hearth, at a *matinee* to-day, and in the regular performance to-night. This will be Mr. Owens' last night, and there are, therefore, only two more opportunities to see this exquisite personation. Mr. Owens has played two hundred nights this season, and his engagement has been a remarkably successful one—the two memorable points in it being his wonderful delineation of Solon Shingle and the delicious performance of the old toymaker. None who have hitherto neglected to see Caleb Plummer should miss the last chance.

Personal Intelligence.

Samuel Downing, one of the four survivors of the Revolution, has arrived at the Astor House, intending, in accordance with the invitation of the committee, to take part in the celebration on the 20th. He is one hundred and four years old, but is quite hale and hearty. His home is at Edinburg, Saratoga county, in this State.

The Seven-Thirty Loan.
PHILADELPHIA, April 14, 1865.

Jay Cooke reports the subscriptions to the seven-thirty loan to-day $3,642,000, including a single subscription of nearly half a million from New York, and large Western subscriptions; one from Pittsburg of $160,000 and one from Chicago of $110,000. The number of individual subscriptions for amounts of $50 to $100 was twenty-five hundred.

Fort Sumter Celebration at Bangor.
BANGOR, Me., April 14, 1865.

The restoration of the old flag to Fort Sumter was celebrated here to-day by national salute at noon, by a display of all the flags on public and private buildings, and by the raising of the Stars and Stripes one thousand feet above the city by means of a monster kite bearing the name of U. S. Grant.

WASHINGTON.

The Cabinet in Counsel on the Reconstruction Question.—The Passes to the Virginia Rebel Leaders Revoked by the President.—General Weitzel Relieved of Command at Richmond.—Arrival of Captured Rebel Officers, &c., &c., &c.

WASHINGTON, April 14, 1865.

EFFECT OF THE DISCONTINUANCE OF THE DRAFT.

The discontinuance of drafting, and other semi-civil military operations of recruiting, will relieve from duty about seventy-thousand persons—provost marshals, enrollment officers, detectives, &c. It is said that in and about this city there are nearly six thousand of these officials, the services of nearly all of whom can now be dispensed with.

REVOCATION OF THE PASSES GIVEN TO REBEL VIRGINIANS.

The President to-day has ordered the revocation of the passes to Messrs. Hunter, Letcher and other leading rebel officials, to visit Richmond for a consultation in regard to the States of Virginia, and a return to its allegiance to the general government. He is willing and intends that a convention for this purpose shall be held, but does not propose that these persons shall be its controlling spirits. The President says that the action of the Military Governor, in granting these passes, was without sufficient authority.

GENERAL PATRICK IN COMMAND OF RICHMOND.

General Weitzel has been relieved of his command at Richmond, and General Patrick has been for the present placed in command at that point. It is said that he was relieved for his action in the matter of authorizing the assembling of leading Virginia secessionists to consider the return of that State to her allegiance, but nothing reliable can be ascertained about it to-night.

MEETING OF THE CABINET.

There was a Cabinet meeting to-day, at which General Grant was present. The subject of pacification and reconstruction was considered, but no determination was arrived at

General Grant expressed the fullest confidence that Johnston would surrender within a few days, if he has not already done so, and it was thought best to await the progress of events.

THE TRADE REGULATIONS WITH THE REBEL STATES.

Important modifications of the trade regulations with rebellious States have been prepared during the past week, but they have not yet been approved, and since the arrival of General Grant, and consultation with him, it is doubtful whether they will be promulgated. It is believed that the work of pacification is proceeding so rapidly that in a very short time it will be possible to remove most of the restrictions and supervision at present necessarily imposed.

GENERAL BUTLER ABOUT TO RESIGN HIS COMMISSION.

General Butler has prepared his resignation of his commission as major general, and will to-morrow present it to the Secretary of War.

ARRIVAL OF CAPTURED REBEL OFFICERS.

J. B. Kershaw, and Brigadier Generals S. M. Barton, J. P. Simms, M. D. Corse, D. M. De Bose and Eppa Hunton, of the rebel army, and Commodores Thos. T. Hunter and J. B. Tucker, of the rebel navy, with some four hundred and thirty other field and line officers, captured by Sheridan, have just arrived by the steamer Cossack from City Point. At about four o'clock this afternoon much excitement was apparent on the avenue in the vicinity of Fourteenth street, and presently a column of rebel officers, in gray uniform, came marching up past the NEW YORK HERALD office, toward the headquarters of General Augur. At the head of the column on the street were one of the ambulances, filled with sick and disabled men of the party. The streets were lined with spectators, and all sorts of rumors were at once set afloat.

"That's General Lee," said one of the knowing.

"Which one?" was inquired.

"Oh, that one on the lead, with the gray mustache."

"Oh, no; that's not Lee, I know him."

"Then it's Ewell," said the wise one, determined to get something right.

On arriving at the Provost Marshal's office the facts proved to be, that Lieutenant General R. S. Ewell and others were invited into Colonel Ingraham's rooms, where they remained for an hour or more, being visited by several old friends. Major Generals Hitchcock and Ingalls called upon General Ewell, who was an old classmate of one and an army acquaintance of both. There were several ladies also admitted to short interviews with the general officers.

A large concourse of people remained outside to obtain a passing glance of Ewell as he left. Just before car time the generals made their appearance, and the column marched down toward the depot. The officers named above were ordered to Fort Warren, Boston harbor, accompanied by their secretaries, while the others were committed to the Old Capitol prison until to morrow, when their cases will be disposed of.

General Ewell and party will be due in New York at half past five to-morrow morning. Major Campbell Brown, Acting Adjutant General to Ewell, was allowed to accompany him. In personal appearance and temperament Ewell is not unlike Gen. Wm. T. Sherman of our army, though his forehead is not quite so broad. He is bald on the top of his head, wears his hair and beard trimmed short, and has a wooden leg. He is very popular with his officers, who saluted him with affectionate respect as he passed the column in an omnibus on his way to the train.

Captain Russell, Assistant Provost Marshal; Captain Forehand, and a guard of the Ninth veteran reserves, accompany Ewell and party to Boston.

THE NEW COLLECTOR OF NEW ORLEANS.

Hon. William Pitt Kellogg, of Illinois, has been appointed Collector of Customs at New Orleans, vice Dennison. Judge Kellogg has held during the last four years the position of Chief Justice of Nebraska.

DEPUTY COLLECTOR OF NEW ORLEANS.

Judge Daly, late delegate from Nebraska, has been appointed Deputy Collector at the port of New Orleans.

APPOINTMENT OF CHIEF JUSTICE OF NEBRASKA.

Hon. William Kellogg, of Illinois, late M. C., has been appointed to the vacant Chief Justiceship of Nebraska.

ARRIVAL OF GOVERNOR OGLESBY.

Governor Oglesby, of Illinois, and staff, arrived here last night. He is on his way to visit General Sherman's army, in North Carolina.

THE MEXICAN EMPIRE.

Some of the foreign journals have reported that it is the intention of our government to acknowledge the Mexican empire. A recent act of the President does not, however, support that assertion; for he has recognized Jose A. Godey as consul of the Mexican republic at San Francisco.

Good Friday.

SOLEMN SERVICES AT THE CATHOLIC, EPISCOPAL AND LUTHERAN CHURCHES.

The anniversary of the crucifixion of our Lord for the redemption of mankind on Calvary's bloody mount was observed yesterday with more than ordinary solemnity. What we have not noticed in many years on the same occasion occurred, and that is, that a great many stores were closed, and business on the part of a large portion of the community was suspended. All the churches pertaining to persuasions that prescribe services for the day were thrown open, and congregations crowded them to their fullest capacity. In the Catholic, Episcopal and Lutheran churches the services were of the most mournful character appropriate to the solemnity of the day. The altars and decorations at the Catholic chapels were draped in mourning, and everything betokened sorrow and grief commemorative of the passion and death of our Lord.

At St. Patrick's cathedral the customary sacrifice was omitted and no consecration of the Holy Eucharist took place. Instead of the Mass the services represented the passion, and lessons and tracts containing predictions of His coming, and types of His immolation on the *cross*, were read, together with the history of the passion as related by St. John, to show how the law and the prophets were verified by the Gospel. After this part of the services, what is called the "veneration of the cross" occurred. This custom is as ancient as Christianity itself, and does not, as some suppose, mean any adoration of an image but of that which the image represents, to wit—our Saviour, who was sacrificed on the cross for man's redemption. At the usual part of the proceedings a very eloquent sermon, appropriate to the occasion was delivered by Archbishop McCloskey.

The services at Trinity and other Episcopal Churches were very imposing. The officiating clergymen were Rev. Drs Vinton and Oglesby, and there was a full choir in service.

EUROPE.

The Europa at Halifax with Two Days Later News.—Our Corunna Correspondence.—The Affair of the Rebel Ram.—Ample Satisfaction Demanded from Portugal for the Insult to the American Flag.—Another Privateer Afloat.—The Niagara and Sacramento Gone to Sea.—British Reports and Hopes from Richmond.—The Amended Tariff in England.—A Papal Warning to Maximilian.—Two English Failures for One Million Sterling.—Active Demand for Five-Twenties, &c., &c., &c.

The steamship Europa, from Liverpool on the 1st via Queenstown on the 2d inst., arrived at Halifax at two o'clock yesterday morning. She has forty-three passengers for Halifax and thirty for Boston.

Her news is two days later.

The Europa experienced strong westerly winds during the whole voyage. On the 12th and 13th a dense fog prevailed. On the 3d at 7 P. M., he signalled an Inman steamer, bound East, lat. 51, long. 14.

The Europa sailed for Boston at half past five A. M.

In the allocutions delivered at the last consistory the Pope expressed surprise and sorrow at the sad events which have recently taken place in Mexico. His holiness hoped Maximilian *would abandon the course upon which he had entered,* and satisfy the just desires of the Holy See. The Pope further thanked the bishops of the Catholic world, especially those of Italy, for defending the religion and liberties of the Church, despite the decrees of the secular authorities.

The West India mail steamer had arrived in England with over two and a quarter millions of dollars in specie. She also brought several captains of blockade runners whose occupations were gone.

The *Epoca* of Madrid states that the Minister of War tendered his resignation and that General Lursundi refused to replace him. A later dispatch says that the Minister of War resigned from ill health. General Rivera succeeded to the office.

The King of Denmark relieved Mr. Helleen, Minister of Justice, of his functions. Helleen represented the alliance between the reactionary and extreme democratic parties. It is supposed that all the members of the late Cabinet will return to their posts. A private Calcutta telegram, of March 27, reports commercial affairs in much the same state as on the 25th, when a slight improvement had taken place. The steamship Cuba, from New York arrived at Liverpool at noon on the 1st inst.

THE REBEL IRON-CLAD.

American Demand for Satisfaction for the Injury from the Portuguese.

A Lisbon despatch of the 31st of March says that the American Minister at Lisbon has demanded satisfaction of the Portuguese government for the firing upon the Niagara and Sacramento by the Portuguese forts. He also requests the dismissal of the commander of Fort Belem and a salute of twenty-one guns to the American flag. The American commanders deny any intention of sailing when fired at, as they were merely shifting their anchorage. Nothing as yet has been decided in regard to the matter.

OUR CORUNNA CORRESPONDENCE.

The Rebel Ram Stonewall Gone to Sea.—The Advantages of the Stonewall.—Lisbon Her Probable Destination.—An English Steamer Sailed with Munitions of War for Lisbon.—The Niagara and Sacramento Gone.—Excitement in Corunna.—Responsibility for the Doings of the Stonewall.—Another Rebel Vessel Afloat.—Burning of an American Ship, &c.

CORUNNA, March 25, 1865.

The rebel ram Stonewall has gone to sea. After all the anxieties and precautions of the past six weeks—after all the twists and turns of diplomacy—after all the watching of the two United States ships of war in this port—the ram has been permitted to go to sea. As I wrote you yesterday she came out of Ferrol yesterday morning with a perfectly smooth sea and not a breath of wind. During the entire day she lay off the coast about five miles, as if waiting for the Niagara and Sacramento. During this time she performed some beautiful evolutions—among others, turning by aid of her double propeller, and making the half circle in less than one minute. She remained in sight till midnight, when she disappeared.

The Niagara and Sacramento remained at their moorings in the harbor of Corunna during the entire day. Twice they had gone out to meet the Stonewall in two different days, when the latter did not have everything in her favor. Yesterday, however, I am inclined to believe that Commodore Craven, whose courage and bravery no man who knows him can doubt, was convinced that it would be but a sacrifice of his ships and men to fight the Stonewall. The speed of the latter has been ascertained to be much greater than was at first supposed, and good judges say that yesterday at times she steamed twelve knots an hour. This is more than the Niagara can make without wind to help her, and yesterday there was not a breath. Then, the Niagara requires wind to turn with any rapidity, and with such weather, in such a sea, her guns not being able to make any impression upon the Stonewall, the Commodore, I am satisfied, consulted his better judgment and determined not to give away the vessels under his command. Why has not the Navy Department (who is the Secretary of the Navy?) sent out a Monitor to compete with this new monster? It has certainly had plenty of time to do this since the news of the arrival of the Stonewall at Ferrol reached the United States.

I do not think, however, that the Stonewall has gone far. Last evening a telegram was received here, stating that a steamer left Liverpool on the 21st, with eight heavy guns, and a large quantity of ammunition for another rebel vessel, and two anchors and two hundred fathoms of chain cable for the Stonewall. This ship was bound for Lisbon, and thither I am inclined to believe, the Stonewall has gone. This evening at sundown the Niagara and Sacramento got under weigh and are bound for Lisbon. It is possible that between here and there they may encounter the Stonewall, and if they do there will undoubtedly be a fight. But I am of opinion that the latter has made directly for Lisbon.

There is a good deal of excitement here to day. For the past four or five days the sole occupation of thousands of the people of Corunna have been to watch the movements of our vessels, and to run between here and the lighthouse in the hope of seeing a fight. They are now of course bitterly disappointed, and the remarks made about our ships are not particularly

complimentary. It is certainly a pity to disappoint the curiosity of the good people of Corunna, but it would have been a greater one to have lost two fine ships and six or seven hundred men.

Our own government, that of France and Spain, are jointly and severally responsible for any future damage which this rebel nondescript may do—our own for not having sent suitable vessels here to cope with her, that of France for permitting her to be built and to leave one of her ports under the rebel flag, and that of Spain for having afforded her every facility for repairing and permitting her to ship men in the port of Ferrol. The Spanish government denies the latter charge, but it is capable of the most positive proof, and it is to be hoped that our government will bring that of Spain to account for it. Mr. Fuertes, our consular agent here, is now actively engaged in preparing the evidence of this fact, and will be prepared soon to lay it before the government.

From the fact of eight guns having been shipped from England, it is altogether probable that another rebel vessel is somewhere about the coast to receive them. It may be that they are to be taken on board the Stonewall and transferred to her sister ship, which is now said to be in one of the West India islands. If these vessels reach your coast, it is to be hoped the Navy department will wake up and send out some proper ships to take them.

Three weeks ago the remains of an American ship, burned to the waters edge, floated ashore near

Malpica, a town about twenty-five miles from here. She was known to be an American ship by her construction and her cargo, which was timber, and much of which was found floating, as well as by an American flag, which was picked up near where she came ashore. No one has been found yet who knows anything of her, and after some little vexation, the authorities have given her in charge of the consular agent at Corunna. It is possible that she was burned by the Stone-wall before she came into Ferrol.

English Accounts.
THE IMPENDING NAVAL ENGAGEMENT OFF THE COAST OF SPAIN.

(From a correspondent of the London Herald.)

I herein hand you particulars and information concerning the Confederate steam ram Stonewall, and the United States frigate Niagara and screw corvette Sacramento, about to take part in a naval engagement off this port. The two last named vessels are at present in Corunna, distant about eleven miles from here. They have both had steam up on board for some weeks past, watching night and day for the appearance of the Stonewall. The excitement here and in Corunna is immense. The sympathy of the Spaniards is entirely with the confederates.

The Stonewall put into Corunna on the 21st of February last, from Bordeaux, having experienced bad weather, and sprung a leak aft, about the 3d of February. She came to Ferrol for repairs in the government arsenal here. About ten days after her arrival here, the Niagara came in, being followed by the Sacramento the following day. After they had been here for some five days, the Admiral commanding requested the federals to leave the port, which they accordingly did, making for Corunna, where they remained at anchor with steam up until the 14th inst., when they weighed anchor and cruised about outside the port for about two days, bad weather coming on they again entered Corunna, and are now awaiting the departure of the Stone-wall from this place, which would have taken place this morning but for the strong wind that is blowing from the southwest. One of the officers of the Stonewall has just informed me that they are to steam out to-morrow morning, if weather permits. Captain Page, commanding the ram, arrived here from Paris two days ago, and immediately requested the permission of the Admiral to allow him to leave the port at any moment. The Stone-wall is an iron plated vessel of about nine hundred tons. having a ram, or prow, forward about twen two feet long. Her armament consists of one three hundred pounder Armstrong gun, worked from an armor plated turret, right in the bows of the ship. She has also another armor-plated turret aft, in which are two seventy pounder Armstrong guns . These three are the only guns she carries She is built on the twin screw principle, engines about three hundred and twenty horse power; nominal speed of vessel about ten miles. Her crew consists of about sixteen officers and eighty men, all told The greater part of them are men who be longed to the Alabama and Florida Captain Page last night called the crew aft, and, after explaining the situation of affairs, said that as the confederacy had no longer any ports in the Northern states, it was useless going to America, so they have made up their minds to conquer or to be conquered. All the yards and topmasts have been lowered, and everything on board put in fighting trim. The men would not turn in last night, but were up the whole night, singing patriotic songs. All on board are sanguine of success, from the captain downwards. It is intended only to fire shells from the large gun. The federals rely entirely on success by running the ram down or boarding her

The Niagara is commanded by Commodore Cravatt. She carries twelve two hundred pounder Parrott guns. Her tonnage and horsepower you have probably by you. She steams about twelve miles, but is very long, and cannot turn round in less than half a mile, whereas the ram can turn round in her own length.

The Sacramento carries eleven two hundred pounder Parrott guns, and has a crew of three hundred men; the Niagara has a crew of four hundred and fifty men. It is the general opinion of people here that if the Stonewall can but lodge one of her three hundred pound shells in either of the federals it will sink them in five minutes.

There are two Spanish frigates waiting to accompany the ram out to sea, in order that no fighting may take place in Spanish waters.

The guns in the forts have been got ready for action in case the federals should attempt to break neutrality

The Admiral of the station sympathizes with the South, and when taking leave of the captain of the Stonewall yesterday said he wished him success from his heart.

The wind is blowing very strong at present: I almost fear the ram cannot leave to-morrow, but will write and advise you later if anything fresh occurs.

Mr Buffum, correspondent of the NEW YORK HERALD, has come from Paris, to witness and report the fight. I will write and give you particulars of the same.

British News from Richmond.

ANGLO-REBEL HOPES OF FUTURE TROUBLE IN AMERICA.

The correspondent of the London *Times*, writing from Richmond on the 4th of March, says:—I am daily more convinced that if Richmond falls, and Lee and Johnston are driven from the field, it is but the first stage of this colossal revolution which will then be completed. There will ensue a time when every important town of the South will require to be held by a Yankee garrison; when exultation in New York will be exchanged for soberness and right reason, and when it will be realized that the closing scenes of this mightiest revolutionary drama will not be played out save in the times of our children's children.

The New American Tariff.

The London *Times* has an editorial on the amended tariff law of the

United States It says:—It is impossible to find an excuse for it Tried by the light of reason, or by the results of experience, it is alike condemned The London *Times* ironically credits the framers of the scheme with peculiar wisdom in selecting the 1st of April for its inauguration.

The United States Navy.

The London *Army and Navy Gazette* says:—The work of the United States Navy has now been accomplished, and it must be confessed that in the hands of Farragut and Por.er the high reputation which the officers and seamen of that power established soon after the national existence of itself has been greatly enhanced.

The Atlantic Telegraph

The French government will probably send one or two steamers to accompany the two that are sent by the English government with the Great Eastern across the Atlantic, at the time of laying the Atlantic cable, and it is hoped that the United States government will do the same.

THE FRANCO-MEXICAN QUESTION.

Speech of M. Ollivier, in the French Legislature, on the attitude of the United States.

[Translated for the NEW YORK HERALD from the Opinion Nationale of March 29.]

I congratulate the government upon the promise made that our troops are soon to be withdrawn from Mexico, and that no more foreign expeditions are to be undertaken. Peaceable progress is preferable to warlike ventures. * * * With regard to the press the government has taken no action. It is certain that during some time past the press has acquired great liberty, being generally able to freely discuss all questions. But this same freedom has been and is intermittent and capricious The condition of the press may be described as liberty tempered with arbitrary rule * * * There must no longer be restrictions imposed upon an instrument which, when monopolized, wields a power incompatible with liberty * * * If the great French revolution had been checked before the desperate days of September, and if the counsels of Bailly and Vergniaud had been heeded, we should have had liberty instead of a dictatorship, and Bonaparte, despite his genius, would have remained on a level with Washington; and if Bonaparte, after having charmed and conquered the world, had known enough to stop in time, he would likewise have founded a lasting work. * * * Notwithstanding the enthusiasm with which the Emperor Maximilian was received, the obstacles in the way of his government have not been removed. He is forced to rely upon foreign forces, and the probability of intervention by the United States seems to aggravate his difficulties. *We well know the doctrine entertained by the United States of claiming to prevent the foundation of new monarchical, or colonial governments upon the vast territory of North America.* The United States have not looked with satisfaction upon our intervention in Mexico, and the accession of the Emperor Maximilian. They have refused to recognize him and their ill will towards him is being constantly manifested. *Juarez is still in their eyes the legitimate head of the government. Being a prey to civil war the United States have not hitherto been able to manifest these sentiments save by protests and reservations, but when the war shall have ended—and it cannot last forever—what will happen then?* It is to be feared that the Monroe doctrine will be then triumphantly executed, and that the intervention of the United States in Mexico will destroy our work there. Should this intervention occur after the departure of our forces we would not be bound to aid the Emperor Maximilian; but were it to take place while our flag remained we should be drawn into a war which the country does not care about and takes no interest in. We could not withdraw in the face of such an occurrence, and the situation would then assume a seriousness that none can deny, and which fully justifies our anxieties.

We should, therefore, urge upon the government to make every effort to bring our troops back to France as soon as possible, and not until they are withdrawn will the country be entirely free from responsibility for the events which may occur in Mexico.

Great Britain.

Parliamentary proceedings on the 30th ult. were unimportant.

In the House of Commons on the 31st Lord C. Paget said that the Admiralty had received no proposal for sanctioning or supporting any fresh attempt to reach the North Pole. He was therefore unable to say what course the government would take if such a proposal were introduced.

Mr. Newdegate put some questions as to the idea of the Pope taking up his residence in England as indicated in some foreign journals.

Lord Palmerston replied that the government respected the Pope personally very much, but for him to come to England would be both an anachronism and a solecism.

The revenue returns for the financial year ending March 31 show a net increase of over £104,000 on the year. Notwithstanding the great reductions in taxation the revenue exceeds by nearly half a million sterling the estimates of Mr. Gladstone.

France.

Weekly returns of the Bank of France show an increase of cash on hand of over two and a half millions of francs.

In the French Chambers, on the 30th, the first of the opposition who debated the amendment, Jules Favre spoke upon the necessity for political liberty, but was interrupted by the President and declined to finish his speech. The amendment was rejected.

The amendment in favor of the liberty of the press was debated, but rejected by a large majority.

It is stated that Napoleon will leave Paris early in May, not returning until November, his physicians having recommended seven months' absence in the country air.

The Bourse is firm at 67f. 45c.

Prussia.

In the Military Committee of Chambers the deputies' amendment was introduced with the object of effecting a reconciliation between the government and Chamber, and proposing a maximum strength of the army of one hundred and eighty thousand men, which was rejected by eleven to eight. The committee also rejected the general military estimates and naval estimates and amendments, thus refusing the whole military and navy proposals of the government.

Austria.

Count Mensdorff had made some ministerial explanation in the Lower House Reichsrath. He said the views of the government on the question of the duchies would be communicated in the Federal Diet on the 6th of April.

As regards relations with Italy, he said the government desired to promote the material interests of the two countries; but that Italy maintained a hostile attitude to the government. He desired to recognize, but must maintain the position of Austria as a great Power.

Commercial Intelligence.

THE LONDON MONEY MARKET.

Messrs. Barings' circular says that a large business has been done in United States five-twenty bonds, and that prices advanced early in the week to 57½ a 58, but have since relapsed to 56½ a 57, the demand being chiefly from the Continent.

On Friday the telegrams per the steamship Cuba were received, and five-twenties again advanced to 57¾ a 58¼. Erie and Illinois Central shares have also attracted attention, and have again advanced.

The Bank of England, on the 30th ultimo, reduced the rate of discount to four per cent. at which there is a fair demand for money. This movement strengthened the English funds, and consols are buoyant and advancing.

Kelson, Tritton & Co., East India and general merchants, have suspended payment. Their liabilities are estimated at £900,000 sterling.

Another provincial bank has suspended—the Portsmouth and South Hants Banking Company. Their liabilities are about £170,000 sterling.

The Birmingham and Joint Stock Banking Company had agreed to take up the business of Atwood & Spooner's bank—which lately suspended at Birmingham—and to pay the creditors eleven shillings threepence on the pound.

LONDON, April 1—Evening.

Consols closed at 89⅝ a 90 for money.

AMERICAN STOCKS.—Illinois Central Railroad, 61½ a 62¼; Erie Railroad, 35¼ a 36¼; United States five-twenties, 57½ a 58¼.

THE PARIS BOURSE.

PARIS, March 31—P. M.

The Bourse is steady. The rentes closed at 67f. 30c.

LIVERPOOL COTTON MARKET.

LIVERPOOL, March 31—Evening.

[The week's market report was received per Moravian.]

The stock of cotton in port is 580,000 bales by actual count, being 13,000 bales below the estimates, of which amount 49,000 bales are American.

TRADE REPORT.

The Manchester market was firmer, with an upward tendency.

LIVERPOOL BREADSTUFFS MARKET.

The market is easier. Richardsson, Spence & Co. and others report:—Flour dull and easier Wheat quiet, and quotations are barely maintained; red Western, 8s. a 8s. 8d. Corn inactive, mixed, 27s. 6d.

LIVERPOOL PROVISIONS MARKET.

The market is downward. Wakefield, Nash & Co. and others report:—Beef has a downward tendency. Pork heavy, and declined 2s. 6d. Bacon firmer and packers demand an advance. Lard dull and easier at 58s. 6d. a 61s. Butter flat and declining. Tallow downward.

LIVERPOOL PRODUCE MARKET.

Ashes easier at 28s. 6d. for pots, and 86s. for pearls. Sugar flat. Coffee quiet and steady. Rice quiet and steady. Clover seed firmer. Jute 10s. a 30s. lower. Cod oil quiet at 57s. Sperm oil—No sales. Linseed oil steady. Rosin very dull. Spirits turpentine quiet at 65s. a 66s.

PETROLEUM.—Boult, English & Brandon report:--Petroleum firm at 1s. 11d. a 2s. for refined; no crude in market.

LONDON MARKETS.

Flour firm. Wheat steady. Iron advancing; bars and rails, £6 10s. a £6 15s.; Scotch pig, 52s. 3d. Sugar inactive. Coffee active at a decline of 1s. a 2s. Tea steady at 10½d. for common congou. Rice steady. Spirits turpentine firm at 67s. Petroleum steady at £18 for crude, 2s. for refined. Sperm oil nominal at £82. Tallow downward at 40s. a 43s. Linseed oil flat.

THE LATEST MARKETS.

LIVERPOOL, April 1 - Evening.

COTTON.—Sales to-day 6,000 bales, including 2,000 bales to speculators and importers. The market is less firm, but quiet and unchanged.

BREADSTUFFS.—The market is quiet and steady.

PROVISIONS. - The market is quiet and steady

PETROLEUM firm at 2s. a 2s. ¼d. for refined.

——o——

POLICE INTELLIGENCE.

Two Men Charged with Arson.— Confession of One of the Prisoners.—They Are Committed Without Bail.

John Schon, a wine merchant, living at 269 William Street, and Christian Schutz, a jeweler, residing at No. 6 Roosevelt street, were yesterday arrested by Officer Barton, of the Second precinct, on a charge of arson preferred against them by Mr. John F. Kauffman, keeping a restaurant at 177 William street. From the deposition of Mr. Kauffman, it appears that himself and Schon bought the lease of premises 176 William street of Mr. Louis Thourout, for which they were to pay $650 for two years from the 1st of May next. Mr. Schon then occupied a portion of the same premises for a wine cellar, and Mr. Kauffman had rented another part of the same building. About two weeks ago Mr. Kauffman informed Schon that he did not wish to go into partnership with him. This seemed to excite the anger of Mr Schon, and on the evening of the 9th inst. the rear part of Schon's premises were fired, apparently by design, but the flames were extinguished before much damage was sustained. Mr. Kauffman subsequently received information which induced him to believe that the defendants fired the place, and accordingly entered a complaint against them. They were arraigned before Justice Dowling yesterday afternoon, when the prisoner Schutz made the following confession in relation to the fire :—

On the Monday before the fire I was in John Schon's wine cellar at No. 176 William Street; I was playing cards with him alone: he said to me that I was a smart fellow, and could make fifty dollars easy : he then said that he wanted to put somebody out of the house, and that if I would set fire to the house he would give me fifty dollars. I told him I would not set the fire : he then asked me if I would help him to do it; I agreed to help him; on Saturday night before the fire I minded Schon's place while he was out and bought two gallons of kerosene oil; he brought it to the saloon in a demijohn; he told me he had two gallons more in the house; it was agreed that the firing should be done about nine o'clock on Sunday night, after the young man had closed up and gone away; at about three o'clock on Sunday afternoon Schon went into the

yard, and on his return told me to go back of the privy and take off the balance of the board which he had partly torn off, and to put the board on one side ; I went out and took off the board ; this board was on the back part of the candy store kitchen ; I went to my room, second floor back room, at about nine o'clock in the evening; Schon told me not to make any alarm until a quarter of an hour after I had seen the smoke from my bedroom; I could see into the yard; my two room mates, Schmidt and Salter, were in bed at the time ; I had my window open watching to see the smoke : as soon as I saw the smoke I became alarmed and awoke my room mates, then I took down my trunk; the next day, when I saw Schon, he told me that I ought to have waited longer before I gave the alarm : before Schon told me the kind of business he wished me to help to do, he said that if I betrayed him it would cost either mine or his life.

Fire Marshal Baker gave the matter a thorough investigation, and on the facts presented to the magistrate he committed the defendants to the Tombs for trial without bail.

***

The Case of G. Manizer.

NEW YORK, April 10, 1865.

To the Editor of the Herald :

In your edition of March 9, 1865, you published an account of my arrest, charged with stealing some $1,786 from a man named Reutter, of 227 William Street, New York, with particulars in reference thereto, which were false from beginning to end. The publication has done me great harm, and the account published undoubtedly originated from the fertile brain of a detective. On Friday last Christiana Ticht, and yesterday Henry Languits were convicted of stealing the money, and were sentenced to the State Prison. The money was recovered from them as they were about leaving the country in the German steamer. I will not trespass upon your space with further particulars. I have lived many years in the Fourth ward, and have a family of grown-up children, and in justice to them as well as myself I ask a contradiction in your columns of the most unjust report referred to.

G. MANIZER, 227 William street.

OUT OF THE DRAFT.

Secretary Stanton's Order and Its Effect.—Day of Rejoicing in the Metropolis.—Wonderful Recovery of the Sick and Disabled.—Stanton the Wonderful Doctor with the Wonderful Recipe.—Order of Provost Marshal Dodge, &c., &c., &c.

There was more joy in the metropolis yesterday than twenty victories could produce, each of them as great, glorious and eventful as the capture of Richmond or the surrender of General Lee with his entire army. The Wall street jubilees were more noisy undoubtedly, but yesterday's exultation was far more satisfactory, though more quiet and less demonstrative. It is scarcely necessary to state that the cause of the general jubilee was the sudden, though by no means unexpected, suspension of drafting and recruiting. The great bugbear of

the wheel of conscription was wheeled into " that undiscovered country from whose bourn " it is to be hoped it will never again return. The poor man sang "*Laus Deo*," and the rich man sang praise be to Stanton, with a feeling almost approaching to religious gratitude. The vision of increased taxation was swept away by a magic dash of the warlike Secretary's pen, and men of peace, with constitutional horror of the sword and musket, breathed free once more, relieved from the dreadful anticipation of involuntary servitude in the ranks of the army. The provost marshals, who, twenty-four hours before, were looked upon as beings entitled to a large degree of respect, and even awe, sunk in public esteem with a surprising celerity, and many people who had been studying how "to get around them " for weeks past suddenly discovered that they didn't care a continental toothpick about Colonel Fry, Major Dodge or any of their assistants. Security is a wonderful supporter of courage, and it was in no way surprising, therefore, that everybody liable to the draft should all at once consider himself justified in being as valorous and defiant as he thought proper. Here is Major Dodge's circular announcing the discontinuance of the draft:—

CIRCULAR NO. 47.

NEW YORK, April 14, 1865.

In compliance with instructions received from the bureau of the Provost Marshall General of the United States, the business of recruiting and drafting will be discontinued in this district until further order. By order of

Brevet Lieutenant Colonel,
RICHARD I. DODGE.

A GOOD SANITARY MEASURE.

Secretary Stanton is the best doctor we have had in this region since the formation of the republic. The entire Academy of Medicine is not to be compared to him. The faculties of all the Esculapian institutions in the country are but a bauble beside him. The splendid recipe which he sent all over the country yesterday, free of cost, made more sick men well than a million of diplomed practitioners could cure in twenty years. People who were lame last week no longer limped, hopeless consumptives ceased to cough, half-blind individuals recovered their sight, and numberless cases of heart disease were relieved from all dangerous symptoms, as if by the stroke of a fairy wand, or by a miracle of Heaven. And all this was effected by the simple reading of the recipe, without any rascally compounding of apothecaries or leeches. Truly, Stanton is not only great in war, but great also in peace, and great in the mysteries of the *materia medica*.

WEEPING AND WAILING.

But there are always some who weep while the rest of the world is glad. This was strikingly illustrated yesterday. The miserable few whose business it has been to fatten on the misfortunes of their fellow beings found their occupation gone. No more recruits, no more substitutes, no more jumpers, no more greenbacks! Alas, poor broker! Thy day has come at last. Weep, with none to comfort, and weep on; weep on, until Doomsday. The unfortunate brokers were ruined. Their offices were untenanted, their tents deserted, and their prospects blasted beyond hope of retrieve. The gay flags no longer floated from their rendezvous, and the alluring drums and fifes were hushed forever. Long were their profits, and long will be their weeping and wailing and gnashing of teeth. Not without cause were their sounds of lamentation raised. For weeks past some of them have been feeding, sheltering and watching their embryo recruits with as much care as an English gamekeeper bestows upon his pet pheasant preserves. One luckless individual brought no fewer than sixteen substitutes into the city yesterday morning. He had collected them from the most distant parts of the State. He had clothed them and paid their traveling expenses, sustaining their courage with liberal "drinks" and more liberal promises. He had done all this not entirely, perhaps, from patriotic motives, but with some distant reference to future hand-money, and at the instant when his labors were about to be crowned with success Mr. Stanton's proclamation, like Aluaschar's foot, came down upon the crockery basket and scattered his vision to the wind.

A PROPHET UNKNOWN TO HIMSELF.

Looking over the advertisements under our "Military and Naval" head yesterday, were to be seen a series of notices for volunteers, substitutes, &c. What a beautiful medicine those literary productions must have been to the minds of the authors on reading them over in connection with Secretary Stanton's order. One of these "ads" is worthy of reproduction. It is as follows:

CAVALRY! CAVALRY! CAVALRY! —Recruits wanted for a regiment now doing duty in Washington city. Apply early, as *this is your last chance*, to ex-Captain John L. Cleary, military headquarters, corner of Broome and Mercer streets.

"This is your last chance," truly. The ex-captain never imagined what a prophesy he was writing when he dashed off those five words—"This is your last chance." He ought to be taken in hand forthwith by some of the spiritualistic gatherings as a prophet or the son of a prophet.

A JOVIAL BROKER.

One broker, of a jovial character, was found among the host of sorrowers. He was like an oasis in the desert, but made the grief of his brethren more horrible by comparison. He had the philosophy to post on his booth the following notice:—

NOTICE

CLOSED IN CONSEQUENCE

OF THE DEATH OF

THE REBEL ARMY.

That broker may live to see better days if he reforms.

BLUNT'S HEADQUARTERS,

of course, presented an unusual spectacle. It had a strange appearance, deserted, as it was, by all save a few officials. The change was in remarkable contrast to the scene witnessed during the four months preceding. The swaggering broker, the reluctant volunteer, the sorrowing relatives of intending recruits, even the policemen, were nowhere to be seen, while outside a crowd had gathered, who viewed with delight the process of loading and discharging the "big gun," which Mr. Blunt had ordered to be fired one hundred times, "and yet one hundred times more," in honor of the suspension of recruiting. Brokers sat sunning themselves outside their closed booths, vexation clearly showing itself on their unprepossessing countenances, while little boys chaffed them with inquiries as to whether "they didn't want a recruit?" and "How are you, hand money!" The order for the cessation of operations as regards volunteering was a bitter pill to all of this class.

A SEVERE CASE.

One man presented himself at headquarters yesterday morning, half mad with disappointment, and anxiously inquired was there nowhere he could get his men taken? It appears he had been feasting a party of five men for the last three days, endeavoring to get them up to the mark, and had spent over $200 in this labor of love. He succeeded in "coming round his men but the evening previous, and intended putting them through yesterday morning; but *"L'homme propose et M. Le President dispose."* His chagrin was unbounded as he saw the prize he had toiled for slip through his fingers. Surely he is to be commiserated. This was but one of the many heartrending cases which occurred, and which justly roused the indignation of that honorable class. One man, who had paid $650 on Wednesday for a substitute, visited one of the provost marshals yesterday in a towering passion, and demanded a return of his money, which request was of course, met with a polite refusal, much to his annoyance.

THE COUNTY AND HER QUOTA.

No one, we presume, is more gratified at the termination of the laborious duties of the committee than its chairman, Orison Blunt, who has done so much towards filling our quotas and preserving us from a forced conscription. All honor to Supervisor Blunt and the committee.

The number of men received in this city under the last call is about eight thousand, or nearly one half of the quota assigned, and about seven hundred substitutes. These, while they count upon our quota, are no expense to the county in the way of bounty, thus creating a fund of saving of nearly two hundred thousand dollars, and as much more to the government. This sum far exceeds all the expenses of the committee from the time of the first organization in July, 1863. Probably in no other way than the one adopted by the chairman could one

half this number of substitutes have been procured.

THE FOURTH DISTRICT.

There was little excitement or little unusual to notice in the general appearance of things about the Provost Marshal's office of the Fourth District yesterday. The order from the War Office, however, had the effect of diminishing the crowd about the door, and changing the countenances of those who were in the vicinity from gravity to gayety. The changed aspect of the office was pleasant to observe. The Provost Marshal was ready still to receive recruits, however, but there were no funds on hand to pay bounties, and so none were enlisted. The orders have not yet reached him to discontinue recruiting, and so his office is still formally open.

THE SEVENTH DISTRICT.

There was quite a jubilee yesterday morning in this district on hearing of the order for the suspension of volunteering Volunteers were plenty, and substitutes could be had "for a song." They wandered about like the pig in the nursery rhyme, requesting somebody to take them; but none could be found to accede to their request. The Provost Marshal's office was deserted; and had it not been for its sign no one would have known it was the same place as a few days previous, beset as it was by intending recruits

A solitary guard sat sleepily on the stairs inside, there being no one for him to watch, while a sound of merriment could be heard coming from the room where but a few days since the click of the draft wheel and the calling of the conscripted were the only sounds heard.

Captain Wagner, in this district, has done his duty. Six hundred and fifty-nine men have been furnished since the last call, and for some time past it has been the head of the list as regards volunteering.

THE EIGHTH DISTRICT.

The deserted appearance presented by the Provost Marshal's office yesterday formed a strange contrast to the bustle for the last few days apparent there. Then the office was thronged by a crowd as varied in its character as the interests represented in it were diversified Volunteers wishing to turn their patriotism to practical account and pocket the liberal bounty offered; substitute brokers, anxious to "earn an honest penny," by any and every means in their power; here and there a drafted gentleman eager to send an accommodating person in his place to win the laurels which fate, in drawing him from the wheel, evidently destined for himself, and well pleased by dispensing a little worldly lucre to obtain the privilege of staying in his comfortable home and confining his experience of the stern realities of war to reading the graphic accounts of the contest in the HERALD each morning before breakfast; clerks, whose pens glided nimbly over forms, rolls, certificates, etc., surgeons so actively engaged rejecting and passing recruits, that, if kept as "reasonably busy" in private practice, would be equal to "striking ile," and, though last not least,

the courteous Provost Marshal, in his quiet and agreeable way, attending to and superintending all. How changed the scene yesterday when our reporter made his accustomed daily call.

Silence there and nothing more.

The crowds had departed, the bounty brokers were absent, organizing a meeting to protest against the interference of the authorities with recruiting; the gentlemen who furnished substitutes were, doubtless, speculating on the future value of gold and what they lost by being in too great a hurry with their representatives, or reading the fast bulletin from Oil Dorado; the clerks had disappeared, and even the Provost Marshal himself had vanished. So that, excepting the man in charge, there was nothing to be seen except the ghosts of the departed, in the shape of vacant desks, empty ink bottles, bundles of papers and the doctor's hat.

At the opening of the office in the morning, however, a very exciting scene occurred. Over forty volunteers, a few of whom had been passed by the surgeon the evening before, presented themselves with a regular rush, as if actuated by one impulse—to receive the greenbacks, but, alas! for human expectations, they were speedily disappointed, for two good reasons. The Provost Marshal, in the first place, had not the funds, and, in the next, he had received Colonel Dodge's order to stop drafting and recruiting. On the receipt of this order the Provost Marshal suspended the extra hands employed in consequence of the late draft, thereby reducing the corps of assistance to the usual number.

The absence of the officials in the evening was owing to the fact that from the suspension of business and the day being good Friday they were indulged with a holiday after two P. M.

THE NINTH DISTRICT.

From Fortieth street to Harlem river there was rejoicing yesterday. More than three thousand families were relieved from the dread of losing some valued member, withdrawn from them to fight

For the great prize of death in battle.

Silence fell upon the Provost Marshal's office, and listless clerks were seen where lately all was bustling excitement. Drafted men in the Nineteenth and Twenty second wards who had just received their notices laughed at their late fears, and Twelfth ward men, who had grown callous to the Damocles' sword suspended over them, brightened up when it was removed. Provost Marshal Dunning, Commissioner Sands and the other officials of the department have done their best to discharge an unpleasant duty in a pleasant manner, but it takes an "unco'" civil man to render skinning palatable even to eels, and the Ninth district, not unreasonably, is glad to be relieved of their attentions.

THE RECRUITING HEADQUARTERS TO BE ABOLISHED.

As an appropriate sequel to the order of Mr. Stanton, it will gratify our readers to learn that the recruiting headquarters of the county in the Park are to be leveled with the ground without delay. The booths and tents will also be swept away, and thus will disappear the last unpleasant traces of the reality of war from our city.

The Ice Monopoly.

To the Editor of the Herald :

Our attention has been called to an "article" that appeared in your paper headed "Ice Swindle." As an act of justice we entertain the hope that you will give our reply the same publicity in your paper as the article of swindling has obtained. The grounds you put forth to justify your attack upon our trade are twofold, namely:—The tremendous quantity of ice laid up, and the great fall in the price of gold That in the face of these things we have doubled our prices beyond that of last year, and that therefore, the public should combine to crush such a swindle by keeping from the use of ice, and calling in the Boston and Portland dealers to our city.

The tremendous quantity of ice laid up is not stored here, but at a long distance from the city. It was laid up at great expense and has to be brought here. There are great loss, delay and labor in collecting family bills. Many of them never pay. All we ask is that the consideration you expect in your own business and that you seemingly allow all others should be given to us. At a great increase of expenditure in wages, transportation and all materials necessary for our business, together with increase of taxation, rents, etc —all these charges have undergone no diminution, nor is there any probability of any material reduction. In reference to the charge of doubling our prices, such is not the fact. We charged families last year fifty cents per hundred pounds; this year seventy-five cents, and families taking small pieces one cent per pound; butchers fifty cents per one hundred pounds. We would here observe that the ice trade last year was the only business that did not partake of corresponding advancement in their relative departments. This arose from the disjointed state of the traders. The results of the year showed the necessity of a more united action as to prices. Hence the charge of combination. In no noticeable point has the expenses connected with our trade undergone any alteration. The butchers are loud in their complaints; but you cannot buy meat from them lower since the decline in gold simply on the principle here presented. Boston and Portland dealers have tried this market on several occasions, and could not meet expenses. Families have never taken ice sooner than they can help and we cannot be affected by that threat.

ICE VENDERS.

——o——

The Alleged Wholesale Theft of Liquors.

To the Editor of the Herald:

My attention was called to an account in your paper on Monday last, of the charge of larceny made against me and others for taking a quantity of liquors from the store of Virgil E. Hillyer, and feeling that injustice was done me in that publication, I ask you to publish this explanation of the transaction.

About the 20th of March last, Mr. Amos Barnes came to me and represented that he was a partner of the firm of J. L. Woolsey & Co., and desired to sell to me, in behalf of said firm a large assortment of liquors, consisting of New England rum, and pure spirits, which he said were in the store of said firm in Duane street, and exhibited to me samples of the liquors. As I was about to start for the oil regions, and desired to take with me a large stock of liquors for sale there, and believing the liquors were cheap, and that I could make money by the purchase, and firmly believing that Barnes' representations as to ownership were true, after some days of negotiation I purchased the liquors on a credit of sixty, ninety and one hundred and twenty days. I took from J. L. Woolsey & Co. a bill of sale of said liquors and gave my notes for the same in three equal amounts, and a lien on said liquor to secure the payment of the notes. At the time I purchased these liquors I had no suspicion that there was any other claim to them, nor that Mr. Barnes was not fully authorized to sell them. I required Mr. Amos Barnes to deliver the liquors to me, and procured storage in Brooklyn for the whole amount. Mr. Barnes undertook to deliver to me the goods, and I suppose for that purpose commenced moving them from the store in Duane street. I had nothing whatever to do with the taking of the liquors. I received fourteen barrels from Barnes, and expected to receive the whole amount purchased, and should have received it if it had been delivered to me. Mr. Barnes still holds my notes for this liquor and claims that he had a right to sell it. Whether he had or not I do not know; but I do know that my purchase was in perfect good faith, and that I have been guilty of no intentional wrong in the premises.

Mr. Randolph Barnes, who is also under arrest, had nothing whatever to do with the transaction, but has most unfortunately been confounded with Amos Barnes, who sold me the liquors, and who took out of the store all the liquor that was removed.

NICHOLAS BROOKS.
NEW YORK, April 12, 1865.

GRANT.

The Execution of the Details of the Surrender.—The Army Taking Position Along the Southside Railroad.—Lee in Richmond.—Rocser and Fitzhugh Lee Refuse to Be Surrendered by General Lee.—Names of Some of the Captured Rebel Army and Navy Officers. &c., &c., &c.

Mr. S. Cadwallader's Despatch.
APPOMATTOX, C. H., April 10, 1865.

My despatch of yesterday was hurriedly closed by the departure of a HERALD messenger for City Point. My despatch of to-day shall be confined to some additional details of the great culminating events of the rebellion, as they presented themselves to me, without much regard to importance or order.

CARRYING OUT THE TERMS OF THE SURRENDER.

The appointment of officers to carry out the terms of surrender were made by both parties during the night, and a conference between Generals Grant and Lee was held on the brow of the hill, one-fourth of a mile north of the Court House, at ten o'clock A. M. General Grant and staff had hardly arrived when General Lee, accompanied by an orderly, galloped up the hill and rode to the side of the Lieutenant General. General Grant's staff, General Ord and staff, General Griffin and staff, General Gibbon and staff, General Sheridan and staff, were all on the ground, grouped in a semi-circular position. The country to the outward was open, cultivated land. The Court House stands on a ridge, or continuation of small hills, extending east and west.

THE REBEL ARMY.

Lee's army lay on a parallel ridge, with a ravine and little rivulet between, nearly north of our forces. The head of his column was mainly composed of trains and artillery. The infantry and cavalry brought up the rear. Consequently but a small portion of the rebel army was visible from the Court House.

A CONVERSATION.

As Lee rode up the hillside on a gallop, General Grant stepped his horse forward two or three rods to meet him. Lee rode squarely up, saluted in military form, and wheeled his horse side by side to the left of General Grant. The two chieftains then entered into a conversation that lasted nearly two hours, until the officers appointed on both sides to carry out the terms of the surrender had reported for duty. The tableau at this time was the finest ever witnessed. The two distinguished leaders of the mightiest hosts of the world sat quietly in their saddles discussing the past, present and future in free and easy offhand conversational style.

During the conference General Lee stated that if General Grant had acceded to his proposal for a personal interview some weeks ago peace would have undoubtedly resulted therefrom. Much of their conversation was, of course, private and unheard. But enough was gleaned to know that Lee acknowledged himself completely beaten, the power of the Southern confederacy utterly destroyed, and any further prolongation of the war a useless effusion of blood. The opinion was universal among rebel officers that Johnson would surrender to Sherman without a battle on hearing that the Army of Northern Virginia had done so to General Grant

THE CONVERSATION ENDED.

Shortly before eleven o'clock the interview between the generals was ended by Lee saluting and riding slowly down the slope, across the hollow and into his camp on the hill beyond. General Grant turned the head of his thoroughbred Cincinnatus towards the Court House, followed by his staff and a large retinue of general officers.

MEETING OLD FRIENDS

Within half an hour thereafter the officers designated by General Lee to carry out the stipulations of surrender arrived, and were accompanied by a large number of noted rebel officers. The large veranda and yard in front was soon filled with groups of Union and rebel officers in earnest conversation. Half the "regulars" on either side found some old acquaintance or West Point classmate among the others, and in many instances the greetings were warm and unaffected. The men who but a day before were seeking each other's destruction now chatted quietly together, recalled the incidents of the past, and gave in their open countenances evidences of honest respect. Almost the first questions from rebel officers were—"Well, what are you going to do with—what are you going to do with us?"

THE EFFECT OF GENERAL GRANT'S TERMS.

The belief seemed widespread among intelligent officers that the United States government had pledged itself to grant no amnesties for the offense of treason, and that they must "all hang together or hang separately." On learning that General Grant had taken no advantage of their necessities and desperate situation, but had voluntarily extended to them the same magnanimous terms offered two days before and refused by General Lee, they expressed themselves exceedingly gratified. Discussion of the matter among themselves seemed to greatly strengthen this feeling. All admitted that their army had no further power of resistance, and that it was compelled to surrender on our own terms. They appeared surprised to find no exhibition of vindictiveness on our part. Judging from their hearty confessions of generous and liberal treatment by us one would conclude they expected to have been chained together as felons to grace the triumphal march of our victorious general.

At first some may be inclined to think General Grant not sufficiently exacting. But no one who witnessed the behavior of the rebel officers and listened to their conversation on the subject could long doubt the wisdom of his policy.

LEE'S ARMY DELIGHTED.

Lee's whole army goes home delighted that they are out of the service, and grateful to General Grant for sparing them all unnecessary humiliation. The moral effect of this on the mass of the Southern people cannot be overestimated.

ISSUING RATIONS.

On Sunday evening Colonel Morgan, Chief Commissary of Subsistence for the armies operating against Richmond, issued twenty-thousand rations of bread and meat to the rebel army, and on Monday was able to add the rations of sugar, coffee and salt.

Mr. J. Walton Fitch's Despatch.

HEAQUARTERS, NINTH CORPS,
ARMY OF THE POTOMAC,
BURKESVILLE JUNCT'N, Ap'l 11, '65.

There is no change in the situation of this corps since the date of my last despatch. The line of the Southside Railroad from here to Petersburg is still under the guardianship of our troops, and the immense wagon trains of the army

are safely conveyed through their midst to the victorious force beyond. Our advance guard consists of Curtin's brigade, located at Farmville—a village about eighteen miles from these headquarters, and containing nearly two thousand inhabitants, nearly all of whom still occupy their homes.

WHAT NEXT?

Speculations are rife, not alone in the camps, but among officers of every grade, as to what disposition will be made of this army, now that the finishing stroke has been administered to the enemy that confronted it. Already the probability of a Mexican campaign is being discussed, and at least three-fourths of the officers that express an opinion regarding the imminence of a rupture with the would-be empire, are anxious to join the crusade against the Power endeavoring to establish itself in our midst, and restore the wearer of the crown to his " native death " and retirement.

AN ARMY OF OCCUPATION.

I hear it stated as probable that Burkesville Junction—the present location of these headquarters—may be constituted a military post for some months to come, owing to its important railroad communications and centrality. It is evident that some extensive system of provost guards or police will require to be inaugurated in the event of the withdrawal of our forces from this vicinity, as the country will remain in an extreme state of unrest and disquietude for months thereafter. No more unfortunate event could happen to the interests of the inhabitants hereabouts than the immediate and total withdrawal of our troops, as stragglers and deserters from both armies, now roaming through the forests contiguous, would immediately organize into extensive bands of highwaymen, and subject the people to all the terrors and apprehension attending the recipients of the visits of the redoutable Dick Turpin "in ye olden time." The amount of private property in this vicinity and along the whole line of the road now receiving the attention and protection of picket guards furnished by this corps is immense, and covers a large area of country. It is this magnanimous and generous attendance to the interests of the inhabitants that is winning them over to the fealty they forsook, and which will, as soon as the brief sting of pride attending their subjection wears off, cause them to look upon the old government and its administers as the source of all success and well-being.

It would be a cowed and spiritless race that took kindly and indifferently the dispensation that has been vouchsafed this unfortunate rebellion; and that there exists a sensitiveness and petulance from the effect of the just though cruel blow which has wounded the pride of its participators is but natural, and cannot be stifled save by kindly approach and gentle treatment

That the great body of the people we find here in the interior experience heartfelt satisfaction at the end of the war I am positive, and that ultimately they will be brought to the grace from which, in an evil hour and amid unfortunate counsels, they fell, I am equally sanguine.

CAPTURED GUNS.

A considerable portion of the guns captured by us in the late pursuit are now being daily received here. Many of them are of very superior make, and are of the Armstrong pattern.

GENERAL GRANT'S BODY GUARD— "FOURTH REGULARS."

This veteran regiment, from whose rank have sprung upwards of twenty generals, in commands in the service of the government and the rebellion, and among whom were numbered Grant and Sheridan, arrived here this evening from the front, upon their way to join the Lieutenant General—whose body guard they are—having marched from Prospect Hill since eight o'clock in the morning—a distance of thirty-three miles. They will probably take the train from this locality to City Point. The regiment is in command of Major Collins.

Prominent among the rumors of a movement of the Ninth corps is the report that it will be sent to Danville, about seventy miles from its present locality. Nothing has yet transpired to corroborate this supposition. Go where it may, the old Ninth corps will never refuse the "wager of battle" with any antagonist courageous enough to confront it.

Mr. S. T. Bulkley's Despatch.
FARMVILLE, VA., April 9, 1865.
THE IMMENSE SLAUGHTER OF THE ENEMY.

The slaughter of the enemy in the

fight of the 6th inst. exceeded any-thing I ever saw. The ground over which they fought was liter-ally strewn with their killed. The fighting was desperate, in many cases hand to hand. There were a number of cases of bayonet wounds reported at the hospitals.

LIST OF REBEL OFFICERS CAPTURED ON THE 6TH.

I enclose a list of some of the rebel officers captured on the 6th: —

Navy.

Admiral Hunter, Commodore Tucker, Captain Simms, Midship-man J. H. Hamilton, Lieutenant H. H. Marmaduke, Master W. R. Mayo, Midshipman C. F. Sevior, Midship-man T. M. Banen, Lieutenant C. L. Stanton, Lieutenant J. P. Clay-brook; John R. Chisman, Master's Mate; Lieutenant M. G. Porter, Lieutenant R. J. Bowen, Lieutenant W. W. Roberts, Lieutenant J. W. Materson, Midshipman W. F. Nel-son, Lieutenant M. M. Benton, Master's Mate, S. G. Turner; Lieu-tenant W. F. Shum, Lieutenant T. C. Pinckney, Captain T. B. Ball, Lieutenant H. Ward, Midshipman B. S. Johnson, Midshipman F. L. Place, Lieutenant D. Trigg, Mid-shipman T. Berein, Midshipman C. Myers, J. M. Gardner.

Marine Corps.

Captain George Holens, Captain T. S. Wilson, Lieutenant F McKee. Lieutenant A. S. Berry, Lieutenant T. P. Gwinn.

Army Officers.

Lieut. Gen. Ewell, Gen. Corse, Gen. Barton, Gen. Hunton, Gen. J. P. Simons, Gen. J. T. DeRose, Gen. Custis Lee, Gen. Kershaw and staff,

Col. C. C. Sanders, 24th Georgia; Lieut. Col. J. C. Timberlake, 53d Virginia; Lieut. N. S. Hutchens, 3d Georgia; Lieut. Col. Hamilton, Phil. Georgia Legion; Maj. J. M. Goggen, Maj. E. L. Caston, Capt. J. M. Davis, Capt. Carwall, Capt. J. W. Walker, A. A. G.; Capt. C. S. Dwight, Capt. McRae Cane, 16th Georgia; Col. Armstrong, 18th Georgia; Capt. L. Bass, 25th Vir-ginia battery; Lieut. Col. E. P. False, 22d Virginia battery, Maj. F. C. Smith, 24th Georgia; Capt. J. F. Tompkins, 22d Virginia; Lieut. H. C. Tompkins, 22d Virginia; Capt. W. C. Winn, 22d Virginia; Adj. S. D. Davies, 47th Virginia; L. W. O. Gatewood, 37th Virginia; Adj. Williams, 3d Georgia sharp-shooters; Lieut. J. L. Buford, Capt. J. L. Jarrett, 69th Virginia; Lieut. J. T. Fanneyhaugh, 20th Virginia battery; Capt. J. A. Haynes, 55th Virginia, Capt. A. Reynolds. 55th Virginia; Capt. J. H. Fleet, 55th Virginia; Capt. V. H. Faulteroy, 55th Virginia; Lieut. W. C. Robin-son, 55th Virginia; Lieut. Thos. Faulteroy, 55th Virginia; Capt. R. T. Cland, 55th Virginia; Adj. R. L. Williams, 55th Virginia; Lieut. J. R. P. Humphries, 55th Virginia, Lieut. E. J. Ragland, 53d Virginia; Lieut. A. B. Willingham, 53d Vir-ginia; Lieut. Col. T G Barbour, 24th Virginia; Capt. W. F. Harri-son, 24th Virginia; Lieut. Col. Jas. Howard, 18th and 20th Virginia battery; Capt. A. Austin Smith, Ordnance Officer; Capt. McHenry Howard, Gen. Custis Lee's staff; Lieut. J. F. Porteous, Ordnance Officer; Maj. J. E. Robertson, 20th battery; Capt. S. A. Overton, 20th

Virginia battery; Capt. R. K. Hargo, 20th battery; Lieut. C. W. Hunter, 20th Virginia battery; Lieut. J. H. Lewis, 20th battery; Lieut. A. G. Williams, 20th Virginia battery; Lieut. B. Scruggs, 20th Virginia battery; Lieut. J. M. Suelson, 20th Virginia battery; Lieut. E. Coffin, 20th Virginia; Lieut. Ferneyhough, 20th Virginia; Lieut. P. F. Vaden, 20th Virginia; Lieut. Col. A. D. Bruce, 47th Virginia; Capt. E. Wharton, 47th Virginia; Adj. S. G. Davies, 47th Virginia; Lieut. G. S. Hutt, 47th Virginia; Lieut. C. Molty, 47th Virginia; Lieut. Col. J. W. Atkinson, 10th and 19th Virginia battalions, Lieut. J. L. Cowardin, Adjutant, 10th and 19th Virginia battalions; Capt. T. P. Wilkins, 10th and 19th Virginia battalions; Capt. T. D. Blake, 10th and 19th Virginia battalions; Capt. R. B. Clayton, 10th and 19th Virginia battalions; Capt. C. S. Harrison, 10th and 19th Virginia battalions; Lieut. J. W. Turner, 10th and 19th Virginia battalions; Lieut. B. G. Andrews, 10th and 19th Virginia battalions; Lieut. T. C. Talbott, 10th and 19th Virginia battalions; Lieut. A. P. Bohannan, Adj. Wilson, 10th and 19th Virginia battalions, wounded; Capt. J. H. Norton, 18th Virginia; Lieut. W. Stevenson, 18th Virginia; Lieut. Jos. Russell, 18th Virginia; Lieut. S. Doridian, 18th Virginia; Capt. D. L. Smoot, 18th Virginia; Col. J. J. Phillips, 9th Virginia; Adj. C. T. Phillips, 9th Virginia; Lieut. W. Roane Ruffin, Chamberlin's battery; Capt. B. E. Coltrans, 9th Virginia; Lieut. P. E. Vaden, 20th Virginia; Capt. J. W. Barr, Barr battery; Lieut. W. F. Campbell, Barr battery; Capt. H. Nelson, 28th Virginia; Lieut C. K. Nelson, 28th Virginia; Lieut. J. B. Leftwith, 28th Virginia; Lieut. J. N. Kent, 22d Virginia battalion; Lieut. H. C. Shepherd, 22d Virginia battalion; Lieut. J. E. Glossen, 47th Virginia; Lieut. R. P. Welling, 12th Mississippi; Chaplain E. A. Garrison, 48th Mississippi; Lieut. Robert T. Knox, 30th Virginia; Lieut. J. H. Marshall, 30th Virginia; Capt. J. S. Knox, 30th Virginia; Lieut. St. George Fitzhugh, Pegram artillery; Lieut. T. L. Roberts, 34th Virginia; Lieut. J. S. Watts, 46th Virginia; J. T. Fowler, 46th Virginia; Maj. M. B. Hardin, 18th Virginia battalion; Adj. W. H. Laughter, 18th Virginia battalion; Capt. W. S. Griffin, 18th Virginia battalion; Chaplain L. B. Madison, 58th Virginia; Lieut. Judson Hundron, Lieut. J. F. Oyler, 58th Virginia; Lieut. John Addison, 17th Virginia infantry; Lieut. Col. G. Tyler, 17th Virginia infantry; Lieut. J. B. Hill, 53d Virginia; Sergt. Maj. J. S. Miller, 20th Virginia battalion; Lieut. M. H. Daughty, 11th Florida; Capt. Winder, Young battery; Lieut. J. C. Murray, Young battery; Capt. W. S. Randall, Gen. C. Lee's staff; Col. J. T. Crawford, 51st Georgia; Col. James Dickey, 51st Georgia; Capt. W. R. McClain, 51st Georgia; Capt. J. H. Faulkner, 51st Georgia; Capt. R. N. Askrow, 51st Georgia; Capt. V. B. Baglow, 51st Georgia; Lieut. J. A. Brown, 51st Georgia; Lieut. C. W. S. Swanson, Capt. H. J. Otis, 2d N. C.; Evans' Brigade; Lieut. P. A. Green, 3d Georgia;

Capt. W. G. Baird, 24th North Carolina; Col. P. McLaughlin, 50th Georgia; Capt. W. A. Smith, 50th Georgia; Capt. E. Fahn, 50th Georgia; Lieut. Thompson, 35th North Carolina; Lieut. Thompson, 35th North Carolina; Lieut. J. P. Percell, 56th Virginia.

INCIDENTS.

From different sources I have gathered a number of interesting incidents, which I give below:

SOUVENIRS OF REBELDOM.

Many have been the souvenirs of rebeldom gathered on this march. A drummer in the One Hundred and Fourty-sixth New York has picked up the major general's commission of General Kershaw. Gen. Mahone's commission was also found. Dr. Lord, surgeon of the One Hundred and Fortieth New York, found seven hundred and fifty dollars in rebel money, and, what is more remarkable, a surgeon's sash, which he presented, after his capture at Chancelorsville, to a surgeon in the rebel army. There were immutable marks on the sash admitting no doubt of its authenticity; besides, its being found in a desk, filled with papers and letters of the rebel surgeon to whom he had originally donated it. Of letters, pistols and sabres, there was no end of appropriation. Among revolvers was a thirteen-barreled one. The most stupendous story of all is finding a twenty dollar gold piece. If the confederacy is not ruined, one man in it certainly is by the loss of this much of suriferous metal. Since writing the above I am told that a box was found containing one thousand dollars in gold, and a paymaster's safe containing two hundred and fifty thousand dollars in rebel scrip.

HEADQUARTERS SIGNAL CORPS.

A brilliant exploit was accomplished during one of the late fights by Captain Renyaurd and Lieutenant Miles, Fifth corps headquarters' signal officers, and the signal corps under them. Advancing ahead of our skirmishers they captured a rebel signal detachment, seven al. together, including a captain, their commanding officer. In addition to this they also captured two naval officers and an engineer on a flying exodus from Richmond.

TO WHAT BASE USES AT LAST.

Our boys got possession of two battle flags. One lay partially concealed in a ditch by the roadside, and the other was one of a heterogenous list of articles stowed away in an old canvass bag, which, with its contents, had been thrown away. We read of base uses and the contingency of the dust of the great Cæsar stopping a rat hole; but here we had a tangible exhibition of an ignobility of end and depth of descending that any modern believer in Southern braggadocio would have believed impossible, unless the aforesaid rebel flags were surrounded by a hecatomb of rebel corpses and dyed with the chivalric blood of their defenders.

GALLANTRY.

Corporal Payne, of the Second New York, captured three battle flags and thirty-five prisoners.

Lieutenant Custer, the General's brother, captured another flag, but in doing so received a severe wound in the cheek; but after being hit he seized the colors, then shot the man who hit him, and escaped, bringing the flag with him.

THE CAPTURE OF GENERAL EWELL.

Gen. Ewell and six of his staff were captured by two men—Capt. Stevens and private James Coppinger, both of Company B, First New York.

THE WOUNDED.

Gen. Mott, while leading the Third division, Second corps, on April 6, was shot in the leg and came to the rear.

Col. Starbird, Nineteenth Maine, was wounded, probably mortally, in an attack of the skirmish line on the evening of the 7th.

The Twenty-fourth Corps and the Capture of Richmond.

To the Editor of the Herald:

RICHMOND, Va., April 8, 1865.

Will you please insert and correct an error which appears in your Twenty-fifth corps correspondent's report of the advance upon and occupation of Richmond? If allowed to go uncontradicted the great credit claimed and justly earned by the Twenty-fourth army corps is carried off by sufferance to the Twenty-fifth corps. The facts in the case are as follows:—The skirmish line of the Twenty-fourth corps, composed in part of the Ninth Vermont and the Eighty-first New York, were at least an hour in the advance of the skirmish line of the Twenty-fifth corps. Captain J. R. Angel's light battery, K, Third New York artillery, closed upon the skirmish line in the advance, and as work after work and

fort after fort was approached the colors of battery K, in the hands of Captain Angel, were planted prominently thereon and then advanced to the next. Finally the city of Richmond was reached, and the colors of battery K were unfurled on the steps of the Capitol two hours and thirty minutes before the colors of any other battery.

When the main body of the two corps moved upon Richmond the Twenty-fourth was also ahead.

JUSTICE.

NEWSPAPER ACCOUNTS.

The Rebel General R. E. Lee Reported in Richmond.

[From the Richmond Whig, April 13.]

We learn that Robert E. Lee arrived in the city last night.

The Rebel Generals Rosser and Fitzhugh Lee Refuse to Surrender.

[From the Richmond Whig, April 13.]

Generals Rosser and Fitzhugh Lee refused to abide by the terms of surrender, it is said, and made their escape, unattended, to "parts unknown."

The Number of Men Surrendered by Lee.

[From the Richmond Whig, April 13.]

The number of men surrendered by Gen. Lee is stated to be twenty-five thousand, of whom only eight thousand had muskets. The rest had thrown away their arms during the forced marches into the interior.

How the Obstacles to the Cordial Reunion of the People of the North and South Are Being Removed by Our Soldiers.

[From the Richmond Whig, April 13.]

Now, when it has become apparent that the Union will be pre-served, and that the Southern States will resume their relations to the sisters whose companionship they renounced in an evil hour of blindness and passion, it is well to consider what obstacles still oppose a cordial reunion, and whether they may not be removed.

Among these obstacles, perhaps none is greater than the idea which has been sedulously inculcated by the designing advocates of discord for many years, that the people of the Northern and Southern sec-tions hate each other with inex-tinguishable enmity, and that this hatred is so deeply founded in the habits, tastes and opinions of the people that it cannot be eradicated. Nothing has contributed more to keep up the resistance of the South-ern people than the teachings of those who declared that the North was inspired with a feeling of en-mity and revenge so bitter that nothing would satisfy her people except the utter ruin of Southern homes, the desolation of Southern families, and the destruction of all that made life worth preserving.

The passions kindled by the war, and the deeds of rapine and viol-ence on both sides to which the war has given birth, have for a long time prevented us from de-veloping the real sentiments of hu-manity and kindness to which thousands will happily return now when the blood-red flames of the conflict are beginning to subside.

We feel sure that even *the most embittered secessionist will acknowledge that the conduct of the United States officers and soldiers in Richmond has* *been not only considerate and humane, but adapted to inspire confidence and kindness in return.* And, with the prospect of returning peace, the sentiments of the people of the North are beginning to appear in forms which ought to elicit corre-sponding feelings.

The prompt action of the Chris-tian Commission in supplying all the destitute among us with food certainly does not savor of a spirit of hatred and revenge. We have heard of various expressions of good feeling from many Northern communities, which will speedily be manifested, we are sure, in more substantial forms than mere words.

When contrasted with the *reck-less spirit of destruction and disregard of private rights and property exhibited by the leaders of disunion*, even to the very hour of their final flight from Virginia, these developments of kindness and sympathy from those who were lately reckoned as ene-mies of the South will not fail to *work a change in many minds.*

We earnestly exhort the people of the South to dismiss rancor from their hearts, to believe what is un-doubtedly true, that their brethren of the North desire to live with them in the bonds of peace, and to culti-vate a spirit of conciliation and for-bearance, which will soon bear the richest fruits.

The Duty of All Virginians to Sub-mit to the United States Authori-ties.

[From the Richmond Whig, April 13.]

The duty of all true Virginians is perfectly apparent. Whatever may have been their previous views and wishes, they will now step forth and acknowledge at once the authority of the United States government, and that they owe full allegiance to it. The slightest hesitation in regard to this matter can but still further complicate the difficulty of the situation and throw additional obstacles in the way of a speedy return to that quietude and freedom from restraint that are essential to enable the people to recover from the blighting effect which this unhappy war has had on every interest in this State. *The course of the authorities and of the soldiers in this city is well calculated to inspire confidence in their desire to see harmony and fraternal feeling restored in our common country ; and we feel confident that our people in every section of the State will freely respond,* and do all in their power to bring about a consummation which will be fraught with so much happiness and good.

IMPORTANT FROM MEXICO.

Surrender of the Chief Army of Juarez in Central Mexico, &c., &c.

CAIRO, Ill., April 14, 1865.

New Orleans advices of the 8th inst. are received.

The *True Delta* claims to have official intelligence that General Rheagena, commanding the chief army of Juarez in Central Mexico, has abandoned the contest. His whole army has given up fighting and returned to their homes.

News from Chihuahua.

To the Editor of the Herald :

NEW YORK, April 13, 1865.

From a letter received from a friend in the city of Chihuahua, Mexico, the following items are gleaned :—

Juarez and his cabinet are still, as they for a long time have been, in that city. The republican forces with the President number about one thousand five hundred men. The nearest imperial troops is a force of six hundred, which has for some time been stationed at the town of Cerro Gordo, in the State of Durango, but quite near the Chihuahua line. They at one time entered the latter State, visiting the towns of Valle and Parral, but making no progress, were soon withdrawn.

A Mr. Leaton, from Passo del Norte, is recruiting Americans for service under the Juarez banner, and has already enrolled about seventy-five. General Gonzala Ortega, of the republican army, passed through the city of El Paso a short time ago, on his way to the United States, on special business from the President. Colonel Heintz, a Hungarian in the republican army, was also in the above mentioned city at the same time, on his way to California, for the purpose of raising a force of a thousand or fifteen hundred men in that State for services under President Juarez.

The enclosed printed slip is an official announcement by the Juarez government of a victory gained by that brave republican partisan leader Corona, over a detachment of imperial soldiers, and has not yet reached us here by the ordinary channels of communication.

**Huzza for National Independence.—
Honor to the State of Sinaloa.—
Thanks to General Corona.**

The government has received the welcome intelligence, officially, that the valiant General Corona, after inflicting considerable loss on the road upon the French forces marching from Durango to Mazatian, has completely defeated one hundred *Chasseurs des Vincennes* (French sharpshooters) at the town of Ver-anos—those who did not fall in action being shot. Particulars are in press, and will be published forthwith.

Chihuahua; Feb. 3, 1865.

—o—

NEWS FROM NASSAU.

Arrival of the Steamship Corsica.

The steamship Corsica, Captain L. Mesurier, from Havana on the 8th, and Nassau on the 10th inst., arrived yesterday morning.

The French bark Eugene of Marseilles, with a cargo of about 3,000 bags of coffee, 2.000 pieces of mahogany (crotch) about 1,200 pounds wax, 1,800 dried hides, and about 30 tons of logwood, was totally wrecked on the northeast point of Great Inagua on the morning of the 25th of February last. The captain and part of the crew were saved; the mate and two seamen were drowned. The blockade runner Banshee, with 1,000 bales of cotton, arrived at Nassau on the 30th from Galveston. She reports Galveston garisoned by twelve hundred troops Twelve Union ships were off the bar. Six steamers had sailed recently from Havana for Galveston.

FATAL ACCIDENT ON BOARD THE STEAMSHIP CORSICA FROM HAVANA.

A terrible accident occurred on board the steamer Corsica, on her late passage from Havana to this port, which resulted in the death of two persons and seriously injuring three others. It appears that, when four hours out from port, a barrel of spirits was about being lowered into the lower hold, when, owing to some wrong management in arranging the slings, the barrel slipped and fell with great force into the hold, where it immediately burst. The storekeeper, Mr. John Hughes, who was in the hold at the time, with several others, upon seeing the occurrence, went immediately to the barrel, and having a lighted candle in his hand, it set fire to the spirits, which exploded, killing Mr. Hughes instantly and mortally wounding the carpenter, Mr. E. McNeal, who died on Thursday night. Three others of the crew, named Mitchell, Thompson and Murphy, are seriously injured, but will recover. The passengers held a meeting on board for the relief of the sufferers, whereupon some eight hundred dollars were subscribed.

———

The War on the Guerillas.

CAIRO, April 14, 1865.

The rebel Colonel Forrest and staff arrived at Memphis, under the flag of truce granted by General Wright, for the purpose of conferring with General Washburne upon the subject of exterminating guerillas. The result of the conference is not known.

SHERMAN.

His Army Moving.—The March Begun on the 9th Instant.—Sherman's First Speech.—Johnson's Army West of Raleigh.—Only His Cavalry Holding the Capital of the State.—He Is Endeavoring to Form a Junction with Lee.—The Ram Albemarle Raised in Good Condition.—Occupation of Murfreesboro, N. C., by Our Fleet, &c., &c., &c.

Our Special Washington Despatch.

WASHINGTON, April 14, 1865.

Reliable information has been received here from Goldsboro to the 10th, instant. General Sherman started from Goldsboro early on the morning of the 10th, moving to Raleigh. There was no fighting except the usual skirmishing. It was General Sherman's expectation that he would reach Raleigh in four days.

Daily communication will be kept up with the army, and the railroad will be repaired at once.

Mr. D. P. Conyngham's Despatch.

NEWBERN, N. C., April 11, 1865.

THE NEWS OF THE FALL OF RICHMOND IN SHERMAN'S ARMY.

Sherman's veterans testified their rejoicings at the fall of Richmond in the most noisy and frenzied manner. At night the men took it into their heads to improvise a general salute by putting powder into hollow logs and blowing them up. This, accompanied by the cheers of the men, the capering of dancing negroes, who appeared to be bit by tarantulas, and the music of several bands, made the scene enlivening enough.

SHERMAN MAKES A SPEECH.

A crowd of soldiers and citizens, accompanied by a band, made a favorable demonstration in front of General Sherman's headquarters. They loudly and vociferously called for the General. He had to make his appearance, and, after thanking the men, said.

" We have glorious news, soldiers. Richmond is ours, and the rebel army is broken up and demoralized. I have a letter from General Grant, in which he says that he is pursuing Lee, and wishes to have us press Johnson, which I think we'll do. (Cries of ' We will, we will.') We don't mean to let him rest, so be prepared for the march in a few days."

Loud cheers were given for Sherman, for Grant and his army, and the men returned to their quarters congratulating one another.

THE ARMY ON THE MARCH.

On the afternoon of the 9th a part of Schofield's column took up their line of march, and yesterday morning the whole army broke camp and debouched from the different encampments around Goldsboro into column along the different lines of march.

ORGANIZATION OF THE ARMY.

The army is divided into three different columns—one under General Slocum, another under General Schofield, and the third under General Howard. The men are in excellent condition and spirits, eager to meet the enemy to wind up "the darned affair."

JOHNSTON'S POSITION.

Johnston's army has occupied a line of intrenchments along the Neuse river, some twenty miles from Goldsboro, but has fallen back within a few days *west of Raleigh*. Colonel Spencer, Third brigade, Kilpatrick's cavalry, sent some orderlies towards Raleigh. They got to the rear of Hampton's cavalry and ascertained that Johnston had evacuated the town, and that it was occupied by four or five thousand cavalry. Hampton had his headquarters eight miles east of Raleigh, on the Smithfield and Raleigh road. Johnston is reported gone to Greensboro, on the junction of the Danville and Charlotte road. It is evident that he is trying to form a junction with Lee, and will then fall back to Western Georgia and Alabama. They have important arsenals at Macon, Columbus and Augusta. They cannot strike for Eastern Tennessee, as Thomas is heading them off there, so their route will be through North and South Carolina and Georgia.

I do not expect immediate fighting, except what the cavalry will make.

STATE OF THE CONFEDERACY.

I have just laid hands on a Raleigh *Confederate* of April 7, in which was Jeff. Davis' last proclamation from his new capital, which I have telegraphed. Though he admits that the fall of Richmond will have a serious moral effect, still he thinks it is in reality no great loss, as it leaves Lee's army free for active operations anywhere. He states that "our army will be free to move from point to point." That is true, for they are now rapidly moving each on his own hook, and giving up the confederacy as a "gone coon."

The *Confederate* goes it strong on the *Conservative*, Governor Vance's organ, for suggesting that overtures for peace should be made to the Union government. There is a civil war in the camp, and it is fast becoming a Kilkenny catawauling affair.

INCIDENTS OF SHERMAN'S MARCH.

Towards the evening of the 10th Major General Howard, staff, escort and some mounted infantry were in advance, when they struck some rebel cavalry, who opened on them, killing a horse of one of the General's staff and wounding some men. The General himself had a narrow escape. His men charged on the rebels, and captured about one hundred and two pieces of artillery.

A PAYMASTER NEARLY CAPTURED.

On the 9th Major Fulsifer was passing from Wilmington to Goldsboro, when he stopped to pay the troops at Burgan, some twenty miles from Wilmington. The troops had moved forward that morning, except a squad of nineteen men, under Lieutenant Colonel Parker. The Major followed up the troops, and towards evening a troop of rebel cavalry swept into the town, gobbling up the little force there and the telegraph operator. They stopped the latter and made him cut the wires. They partially injured the bridge.

THE CONDITION OF SHERMAN'S ARMY.

When Sherman struck Goldsboro the army was shoeless and ragged, but they are now thoroughly clad and refitted. Brigadier General Easton, who is chief quartermaster to the army, was busily engaged hurrying forward supplies, while Sherman was making his sweeping march from Savannah. He had established depots at Beaufort, Morehead City and other points, and as soon as Sherman reached Goldsboro supplies were rapidly forwarded to him. Several hundred cars were plying backward and forward, and when the army started it had thirty days' rations on hand and such a surplus of clothes that some had to be returned.

As supplies are the sustaining power of an army, too much praise cannot be bestowed on General Easton for his indefatigible and successful administration.

COLONEL WRIGHT,

Chief Engineer of Railroads, has done much in assisting the Quartermaster's Department by the rapid manner in which he put the railroad in order. The railroad from here to Goldsboro is as safe for travelling purposes as any of the New York lines.

Tracks were laid, bridges built and communication opened with wonderful celerity, under the management of Colonel Wright.

As we are going to keep a base open, it is of the utmost importance to have such men at the head of affairs.

There have been some changes made in commanders. Colonel Patrick Jones has returned from New York, with the well merited rank of brigadier, to his brigade, Second brigade, Second division, Twentieth corps. Few officers have done more to merit a star than General Jones.

Colonel Mendel, Thirty-third New Jersey, has been appointed chief of General Slocum's staff, ranking as brigadier.

Colonel Schofield, brother of General Schofield, has been appointed brigadier general and chief of his brother's staff.

Brigadier General C. C. Wolcott has been promoted from the command of a brigade to the command of the First division, Fourteenth army corps.

Captain John L. Hover has been promoted to a majority.

Captain Hovey and two men captured seventy-eight men and officers near Goldsboro. He struck on them, persuaded them that they were surrounded, and actually frightened them into a surrender.

Lieutenant L. B. Mitchel, ordnance officer, Fifteenth army corps, promoted to be captain and aid on General Ayres' staff.

Major Max Woodhull, Adjutant General, Fifteenth army corps, has been promoted to a lieutenant colonelcy.

Lieutenant W. H. Barlow, Quartermaster, promoted to a captaincy and assistant quartermaster.

Captain Montgomery Rochester, Assistant Adjutant General on General Sherman's staff, has been assigned to duty as assistant adjutant general of the army of Georgia, General Slocum commanding. This will give Captain Rochester the silver leaf. Captain Rochester is an old and distinguished officer, having been all through the war from the first Bull Run fight. The Captain well deserves his promotion.

Brigadier General Webster has just returned to Newbern from the front. General Webster, as Chief of General Sherman's staff, is about establishing his headquarters at Newbern. The General's reputation and executive abilities are too well known to need any comment. During Sherman's important Atlantic campaign he ably managed the bureau at Nashville.

Captain W. R. Tuttle accompanied the General. He is chief of conductors on the military railroads. His efficient services in Tennessee are sufficient guarantee that the military management of the railroads in North Carolina will be ably conducted.

General Charles Crufts and staff have returned from his command of the detachments of the army of the Cumberland which had been left in Tennessee, and which he brought out to the command of his division.

THE REBEL RAM ALBEMARLE.

The celebrated rebel ram Albemarle has been raised by Messrs. Underwood & Co., and is now lying in North river, at the mouth of the canal, waiting to be towed into Norfolk. They have been nearly one month in getting her up. It will be recollected that this monster was blown up by a torpedo, on the 27th of October, 1864, by Lieutenant Cushing and eleven men.

She is not seriously injured. Much of her plating had to be removed to lighten her. Her guns, which were two one hundred-pounder Brook rifle guns, English manufacture, had been taken off by Captain Macomb, in charge of the fleet, and sent to Washington. Her boilers and machinery are unin-jured, and she is at present under steam. The Albemarle was one of the most formidable rams of the confederacy, and was built at Halifax, N. C. She has several indentations in her sides from the different shots and shells fired into her, and an unexploded shell was found buried under her iron plating. She had twenty-eight inches of timber and four inches of plating. She is a regular leviathan, and can be put in full repair at a very small cost. In her were found officers' clothing, arms and twenty eight cans of powder uninjured. She had Liverpool coal on board, which must have run the blockade.

THE LAST OF THE REBEL RAMS.

The new rebel ram, which had been building at Halifax, and was anxiously expected to commence operations, was discovered on the 8th instant, near Plymouth, a regular shell, having been burned to the waters edge. The pickets near Plymouth saw her coming down the river and gave the alarm. Colonel Fronkle turned out a squadron of cavalry and two sections of artillery to charge on her, but they found her helplessly lying against the obstructions, where they placed guards over her, where she now remains. Thus died the last of the rebel rams.

AN EXPEDITION TO MURFREESBORO, N. C.

The Shamrock flagship, Commander Macomb; the Wychusing, Valley City and Hunchback went up the Chowan river to Winston, with the intention of covering the crossing of a body of cavalry at Winston, which was to operate towards the Weldon railroad. The cavalry advance guard found the enemy in position at Winston, but the fleet opened on them, soon scattering them. The fleet then ferried over the troops to the south side of the river, and then proceeded to Murfreesboro, on the Meherrin river, about eighteen miles from Weldon. The sailors took possession of the town, the Mayor formally surrendering it to Commander McComb.

Next day the cavalry charged about twenty-five rebel cavalry into the town and captured them.

Murfreesboro is a good sized town, and is taken possession of now for the first time by the Yanks. The fleet returned to Winston and Plymouth, where it is now lying.

Our Newbern Correspondence.

NEWBERN, N. C., April 10, '65.

THE ARMY UNDER ORDERS TO MOVE.

Some portions of Sherman's army received orders three or four days ago to be in readiness for marching orders, and it was the original intention that the army should move on the 7th. Grant's successes, however, have somewhat changed the programme, and, although the time of moving is delayed a day or two, yet there will not be much difference in the results. Some of the army, the Seventeenth corps particularly, were to have commenced moving this morning, and as Johnston is now said to be making off in the direction of Danville and Hillsboro, and Grant is pushing in the direction of Lynchburg or Danville (at this writing), of course

Sherman will also take a step in that direction.

Since the burning of the vessels on the Neuse river a few mornings since, no further demonstrations have been made on our communications. That was an insignificant affair, comparatively, and a small guard could easily have prevented it. The raiders also burned the upper works of the steamer Mystic, which was sunk in the river a fortnight since. All but her upper works was under water, and her damage, therefore, is slight. It is also reported that the small steamer, General Shepley, was burned at the same time, but I have not heard this confirmed as yet These interruptions do not interfere at all with the sending forward of supplies.

I mentioned in my last that General Howard had established his business headquarters here, although the General himself has returned to the front. Since then General Easton, Chief Quartermaster Military Division of the Mississippi, has also removed his headquarters to this place, and General Beckwith, Chief Commissary of Sherman's army, has also done the same. General Sherman's business headquarters (aside from his field headquarters at Goldsboro) are also to be established here, having arrived yesterday. These straws, together with the fact, that other prominent officers connected with Sherman's army are establishing themselves here, are taken by many as indications that this is to be continued as a base for some time yet, with perhaps Raleigh as the extreme inland base after it is taken, if Sherman chooses to move on that line.

TRAINS TO GOLDSBORO.

Two regular trains are running daily now to Goldsboro, and generally one or more extra trains additionally. The road is open also direct to Wilmington from Goldsboro, and trains are making those trips every day. Some very good passenger cars that were captured by General Terry at Faison's depot, when he was on the march to join Schofield and Sherman, are now being used by us between here and Goldsboro, and between the latter place and Wilmington.

THE OLD STEAMER LONG ISLAND REBUILT.

Lieutenant Bradley, to whom Captain Wing, Chief Quartermaster of this post, has assigned a good portion of the duties that formerly devolved upon Captain Kimball, promoted to the position of depot quartermaster for Sherman's army at this point, relaunched the old Long Island last Saturday. She was a sidewheel steamer that was partially burned a year or so ago, and has been rebuilt in the government yard here. The launch was a successful one, and the boat is, or will be, a credit to the workmen whom Lieutenant Bradley keeps employed in the boat building department.

THE WHITE AND BLACK NORTH CAROLINA REFUGEES.

The number of white and black refugees that are coming in here now by the railroad, from the country surrounding Goldsboro and this

side of there, is immense. The whites are generally of a class who have evidently seen better days. Some of them bring along a few articles of furniture, and perhaps a poverty-stricken cow or horse, but no contrabands. The latter have learned to look out for themselves, and from the number of old beds, chairs, cooking utensils, and rubbish of every description that they bring in with them, one naturally infers that they have also learned to look out for something else besides themselves. The negroes have had a new camp established for them, a little way outside of the fortifications surrounding the town. They are given land to work and materials to work with, and they generally manage to support themselves pretty comfortably. When the males are able-bodied they are given work on the railroads, or by the quartermasters in some of their departments. The whites are mostly taken care of, when they desire it, by Dr. Page, superintendent of white refugees, and also chief agent here of the Sanitary Commission. The doctor rations them and secures employment for them when it is possible. The town is filling up with these whites, some of whom have lived here before, but who return to find Uncle Samuel in possession of their property, and no rent coming from it, of course. Others, who have lost their all, have come hither to get nearer the sea coast, in the hopes of finding the staff of life plentier, or of discovering some more quiet spot than they have been living in under the despotism of Jeff. Davis. Poor creatures, with all the past against them they are to be pitied beyond anything I could say for them. Of the blacks there must be fully fifteen thousand in the city and adjoining it in the outskirts. They reconcile themselves to their new situation more readily, and attribute all their troubles to the goodness of "Father Abraham," and their Maker, both of whom they devoutly believe to be working out the problem of their deliverance.

A CURIOUS ARMY MAIL.

Mr. Chas. Hibbard, our assistant postmaster in this city, informs me that a few days since they sent off a mail from Sherman's army which numbered two hundred and thirty thousand letters and packages. The "bummers" evidently know how to read and write. The mail from that army averages about sixty thousand at every departure. It is a curiosity to look at some of the packages, which are certain to be sent to the dead letter office, they being contraband of the mail.

Fifteen hundred of Wheeler's cavalry came into Goldsboro yesterday, it is said, and surrendered themselves prisoners of war.

Our Goldsboro Correspondence.

GOLDSBORO, N. C., April 7, '65.

A report has just been received from Raleigh, stating that Governor Vance will call the Legislature together for the purpose of repealing the act of secession, and restoring North Carolina to the Union.

The Charge Against Gen. Carrington.

CINCINNATI, April 14, 1865.

Gen. Carrington has published a card, saying that the charges against him are all infamous attempts to obliterate the credit of his services in Indiana. His friends say the matter grew out of a misunderstanding with paymasters, and that all the money for which he is responsible is deposited in the bank, ready to be handed over.

Died.

CARTER.—On Friday evening, April 14, ELIZABETH, relict of Samuel Carter, in the 83d year of her age.

The relatives and friends of the family are respectfully invited to attend the funeral, from her late residence, No. 701 Second avenue, near Thirty-eight street, on Monday afternoon, at one o'clock.

Philadelphia papers please copy.

KEARNEY.—At Nashville, Tenn., on Saturday, April 8, SUSAN, wife of the late Edward Kearney, of Carndonagh, county Donegal, Ireland.

Notice of the funeral hereafter.

Morris Schwalbe,

* * * * * IMPORTER, * * * *

MERCHANT TAILOR

AND DRAPER.

All Work made of the Best Material and in the Latest Styles.   Satisfaction Guaranteed.

1579 THIRD AVENUE

Third door below 89th Street, East Side,

NEW YORK.

ALBERT FRESE & SON,

EXCELSIOR

✳ MARKET ✳

Choice Beef,

Pork, Mutton,

Lamb, Veal.

Long ✳ Island ✳ and ✳ Philadelphia ✳ Poultry.

1231 BEDFORD AVENUE,

Near Fulton Street, **BROOKLYN.**

William Marquart,

GROCER · AND · WINE

MERCHANT

— AND DEALER IN —

PURE FOOD PRODUCTS.

1165 & 1167 Fulton Street,

NEAR FRANKLIN AVENUE,   **BROOKLYN.**

TELEPHONE, 47a BEDFORD.

A. Siegel & Sons,

TAILORS

AND

IMPORTERS

1266 & 1268 BROADWAY,

Between 32d and 33d Streets,

NEW ✳ YORK.

*For well made Garments, Stylish Cut and
Perfect Fit at Moderate Prices,
we are the People.*

GREEN, THE HATTER

1455 THIRD AVENUE,

Near 82d Street, East Side.   NEW YORK.

Very Good Derby Hat, $1.50 & $2.00.

Best Derby Hat, $2.50 & $3.00.

Fine Silk Hat, $3.00 to $6.00.

ABSOLUTELY THE BEST $2.00 DERBY HAT IN THE CITY.

GREEN, The Hatter

1455 THIRD AVE.,

NEW YORK.

BUY YOUR   BUY YOUR

COAL

~~~ OF ~~~

CARGILL,

200 East 14th Street.

EVERY VARIETY,
BEST QUALITY,
LOWEST PRICES,
~~~ BY THE TON OR CARGO. ~~~

100 lb. Bags of Coal delivered to your room, any floor.

English Cannel, Tons or 100 lb. Sacks.

WOOD, CORD OR LOAD.

CARGILL, THE COAL DEALER,

OFFICE,	YARD,
200 East 14th Street, cor. 3d Ave.	From 430–438 East 18th Street.

www.ingramcontent.com/pod-product-compliance
Lightning Source LLC
Chambersburg PA
CBHW020329090426
42735CB00009B/1459